PIMLICO

528

THE FUTURE OF THE PAST

Peter Martland is a research associate in the
Faculty of History at Cambridge University
and a lecturer in history at Pembroke
College external programmes. He is primarily a modern economic historian with
specific interest in the music industry and
media history. He also teaches and writes
about the history of British intelligence. His
recent publications include *Since Records
Began: EMI – The First One Hundred Years*.

THE FUTURE OF THE PAST
Big Questions in History

Edited by

PETER MARTLAND

PIMLICO

Published by Pimlico in 2002

2 4 6 8 10 9 7 5 3 1

Selection copyright © Peter Martland 2002
Individual essays copyright © each author 2002

The editor and contributors have asserted their right
under the Copyright, Designs and Patents Act 1988
to be identified as the editor and authors of this work

First published in Great Britain by
Pimlico 2002

Pimlico
Random House 20 Vauxhall Bridge Road,
London SW1V 2SA

Random House Australia (Pty) Limited
20 Alfred Street, Milsons Point, Sydney,
New South Wales 2061, Australia

Random House New Zealand Limited
18 Poland Road, Glenfield
Auckland 10, New Zealand

Random House (Pty) Limited
Endulini, 5A Jubilee Road, Parktown 2193, South Africa

The Random House Group Limited Reg. No. 954009
www.randomhouse.co.uk

A CIP catalogue record for this book
is available from the British Library

ISBN 0–7126–6856–X

Papers used by Random House are natural,
recyclable products made from wood grown in sustainable forests;
the manufacturing processes conform to the environmental
regulations of the country of origin

Printed and bound in Great Britain by
Biddles Ltd, Guildford and Kings Lynn

Contents

PETER MARTLAND

Preface

The genesis of *The Future of the Past*, like its companion *Globalization in World History*, edited by Professor Tony Hopkins and published by Pimlico in 2001, lies in a remarkable series of lectures given during the academic year 1999–2000 by members of the History Faculty at Cambridge University to mark the start of the new millennium. The purpose of these lectures was to examine a range of broad historical themes and ideas and attempt to place them into some kind of perspective, at what was seen as a defining moment in time. To achieve this ambitious agenda the History Faculty invited a number of its senior members, each a leading authority in their chosen field, to produce a lecture. The core audience were Cambridge history students, together with academics, members of the University of the Third Age and others.

Some time after the lectures were given it was decided to publish them as part of the Faculty's contribution to current historical debates: the first time ever the Cambridge History Faculty has collectively published a book. The result is both *Globalization in World History* and this present volume, *The Future of the Past*. This book differs fundamentally from its companion, which, as its title suggests, focuses on the single but vitally important theme of globalization. In contrast, *The Future of the Past* highlights historical themes and ideas, some of which are timeless and others are not. Both works come together in helping to set a benchmark of where the Cambridge History Faculty is at the start of the twenty-first century. Given our own dismissal of those predictions made by historians, writers and others who, in 1900, were tempted to peer into the unknown, this work is inevitably something of a hostage to fortune. Perhaps a reprint in the year 2050 or 2100 will bring about wry smiles on the faces of those who read it, or perhaps some respect for the ideas of those who, in the year 2000, tried to understand a complex past and to place it in perspective.

Although this attempt at providing a collective showcase of current historical thinking proved reasonable and rational, an utterly unforeseen feature has since entered the equation. For, far from the new millennium bringing peace and prosperity, the world has instead been convulsed by the 11 September 2001 attacks on the United States by the al–Qaeda terrorist network; attacks which have triggered a new kind of conflict, this time a war against terrorism. When the Millennium Lectures were delivered no one could have possibly realised the prescience of the many ideas and perspectives offered by our contributors. For each of these essays contains something to help our understanding of the factors that led to the 11 September attacks, and, of equal importance, help to place in perspective the societies and cultures we now find ourselves defending, as well as the individuals, groups, societies and cultures that now appear determined to destroy our own.

This book has been the work of many individuals, not least our contributors, whose kindly disposition towards this editor has been greatly appreciated. My grateful thanks must go to the Cambridge University History Faculty and especially to Liz Hozier, whose admirable secretarial support went well beyond the call of duty. Thanks must also go to the General Board officer attached to the Faculty, Julian Evans. The Millennium Lectures project was the brainchild of Professor Christopher Andrew, who was Chair of the Faculty during the millennium year. Without his drive and encouragement this book would never have seen the light of day. I must also thank his successor as Faculty Chair, Professor Martin Daunton, who took on the burden of ensuring the project came to fruition. Finally a word of thanks must be offered to the editorial team of Pimlico, whose enthusiasm and encouragement ensured that even the most flexible of timetables could be met.

Peter Martland
Cambridge, 2002

CHRISTOPHER ANDREW

Introduction

This volume has its origins in the series of Millennium Lectures and conferences organised by the Faculty of History (of which I was then Chair) at Cambridge University during the academic year 1999–2000. All looked at major contemporary issues in long-term historical perspective. Such an approach is, of course, straightforward common sense. But this sort of common sense, as Mark Twain once remarked, is nowadays uncommon. Among the distinguishing (though not, of course, universal) vices of the late twentieth century, still present at the beginning of the twenty-first, were its short-termism and short attention span – as manifested, for example, in the increasing substitution of the sound-bite and the instant opinion for reasoned argument and considered judgement. No previous period in recorded history has been so persuaded of the irrelevance of the past experience of the human race. Because the strange new short-term world of the sound-bite and instant opinion has no historical perspective, it has no sense of how bizarre it would have seemed to previous generations – and will seem to future generations. In the long term its sheer absurdity will condemn it to oblivion. Sound-bite culture will one day go the way of Ninja Turtles, Hoola Hoops and other ephemeral nonsense. The dialectic of historical development will see to that. But, in the meantime, there is a price to pay for the Historical Attention Span Deficit Disorder (to use the correct medical term) which currently dominates the political, and even some of the intellectual, culture of our time.

Long-term historical perspective, as Quentin Skinner argues below, helps to 'liberate us from the parochialism of our own forms of

cultural analysis and criticism'. The first great international crisis of
the twenty-first century, provided by the terrorist attacks of 11
September 2001, provided further evidence of how historically
parochial much contemporary conventional wisdom about threats to
global security had become. The nature of the terrorist threat at the
beginning of the twenty-first century was so widely misunderstood
largely because it was seen in too short-term a perspective. During the
previous generation it was increasingly believed that the contemporary
terrorist's prime objective had become publicity rather than victims,
to terrify rather than to kill in the pursuit of political aims. Terrorism
of limited aims, however, was simply a short-term deviation from a
much more dangerous longer-term tradition of terror, of which al-
Qaeda is merely the latest example. As Bruce Hoffman has shown,
historically most terrorism has been far more concerned to kill than
terrify – to destroy opponents rather than to extract political
concessions from them. Until the nineteenth century terrorism was
essentially Holy Terror. Though the word terrorism itself did not yet
exist, a series of religious or cult-based terrorist groups have left their
mark on the English language. The word 'assassin' derives from
Shi'ite terrorists during the Crusades; 'thug' from cult terrorists who
operated in India from the seventh to the nineteenth centuries; 'zealot'
from the millenarian Jewish terrorists of the first century AD.

Like terrorism before 11 September, contemporary understanding
of globalization (a complex concept crudely reduced in sound-bite
culture to the status of a slogan) has been distorted by lack of long-
term historical perspective. There is nowadays a widespread illusion
that globalization is both a recent and wholly Western creation. That
illusion will not survive a reading of the companion volume to this
book, *Globalization in World History* (Pimlico, 2001), edited by A.G.
Hopkins and similarly based on the Cambridge Millennium Lectures
and conferences.

One of the concepts which sufferers from Historical Attention Span
Deficit Disorder find most difficult, if not wholly impossible, to grasp
is that there are occasions when a knowledge of what happened a
thousand years ago gives us a better understanding of current
problems than anything that happened in the twentieth century.
Today's East–West divide in Europe, for example, has more to do
with what happened in the fourth century than in the twentieth. It

reflects not the Iron Curtain of the Cold War but the division between Catholic and Orthodox Christianity which followed the establishment of Constantinople as the New Rome in AD 330 and was made permanent by the Orthodox–Catholic breach of 1054. Though the Orthodox East was later invaded by Islam and the Catholic West subsequently fractured into a Protestant minority and a Catholic majority, the cultural divide between East and West grew stronger as the centuries passed. It is precisely because the East–West divide is so deeply entrenched that it is so difficult to overcome. The new members of NATO who were formerly members of the Warsaw Pact, like those states who are now most likely to join the European Union, are all on the western side of the ancient East–West divide.

Lack of long-term perspective distorts our view of the future as well as our understanding of the present. Most historians are too conscious of the failings of past prophets to wish themselves to prophesy. A merciful Providence allows us, even with the advantage of historical hindsight, to foresee the future only as Saint Paul glimpsed what awaited him in heaven – 'through a glass, darkly'. Were it otherwise, we might lack the courage to confront all the trials which await us. But though the past record of the human race, like our own personal experience, gives us no off-the-peg solutions to the problems of the twenty-first century, it provides insights which we ignore at our peril. Without these insights we have little prospect of distinguishing short-term deviations from long-term trends. We cannot hope either to understand the twentieth century or to glimpse what awaits us in the twenty-first unless we view both in long-term historical perspective. As Sir Winston Churchill put it, 'The further backwards you look, the further forward you can see.'

Christopher Andrew
Professor of Modern and Contemporary History
University of Cambridge

JONATHAN RILEY-SMITH

Religious Authority

Forty-two per cent of the world's population is either Christian or Muslim. The leaders of their great organized – or rather, as will become apparent, disorganized – religions commonly identify secularism and materialism as the greatest threats to them. They are surely wrong. The collapse of communism has exposed the roots of secularism and as they have withered Christianity and Islam have revived, strengthened by the discrimination and persecution their adherents suffered in the past. Materialism is supposed to triumph where religion has failed, but that does not take account of the fact that the most successful materialist country in the West, the United States of America, is also one of the most religious. In this lecture I will argue that the chief problem Christianity and Islam face is an internal one. They have both been grappling with it for the last millennium and are no nearer finding a solution to it than they were in the year 1000. A redeeming feature of the pessimistic account I have to give is that the ordinary faithful, unless unlucky enough to be living under a particularly harsh regime or in a polarized community or caught up in a heresy hunt, have been able to get on with their own modified versions of what their leaders are convinced is the real thing.

Christians and Muslims believe in an interventionary God who has revealed something of his nature, his intentions for mankind and the future of the created cosmos through prophets and inspired scriptures and, in the case of Christianity, through a personal intervention in human history. Given such a belief it is, of course, vitally important to decide what God's messages are, particularly as they are expressed through a medium, the written word, which is notoriously difficult to interpret. This is as true of the Gospels as it is of the Old Testament and of the Koran. There are ambivalences which have to be clarified and contradictions which must be resolved. Divine revelation, moreover, has never been comprehensive. Large areas of knowledge, relating to faith and morals, have not been directly addressed – the Koran itself points out that God chose to reveal to Muhammad only part of a much larger kitab[1] – although certain principles can be deduced which can be applied in cases for which no direct rulings can be found.

But who decides how the ambivalences should be clarified and the contradictions resolved and what the principles are which can then be universally applied? This was an issue in Christianity from the start. The nature of the quicksands on to which scholars had ventured was brought home to them in a series of bitter disputes over the nature of Christ which overshadowed the fourth, fifth and sixth centuries. Was Christ both God and man and, if so, how could this belief be reconciled with the general conviction that there could only be one deity? Was he made by God before time began as an instrument for the creation of the cosmos, so that, although unique as God's one direct creation, he was not God himself, but an intermediary? Or were there in him two separate persons, one divine and the other human? Or did he have only one nature, the divine? Or was he one person with two natures, being at the same time the one God and a true human being, who had risen from the dead and had preceded the rest of mankind to heaven? And how could a religion that claimed to be monotheistic take on board the evidence that Christ had spoken of a third divine element, the Holy Spirit?

It was believed that Christ had given the church the function of teaching and therefore of speaking authoritatively when interpreting scripture, defining the faith and pronouncing on the morality or otherwise of human actions. The decision-making instruments employed by it in this situation, general councils of bishops theoretically from all over Christendom, enabled most Christian leaders to reach a position on which they could – or could be forced to – agree. But a fault-line, which was to open up in the second millennium, was exposed in the aftermath of the conciliar debates. On the one hand the Greek bishops, looking to the patriarch of

Constantinople for leadership now that the patriarchates of Alexandria, Antioch and Jerusalem had been overrun by Islam, seized on the conciliar decrees like drowning men who had come across a raft at sea. The eastern bishops had comprised most of those attending these councils and the doctrinal issues had involved them most directly. For them the decrees of the first seven general councils, the last of which had met in 787, became a framework of belief and a prime source of authority, providing the Orthodox churches with a very firm doctrinal base, although, because many important issues had not been covered, a large area relating to faith remained undefined. Although this meant that differences of opinion on matters about which there was no conciliar decree were generally tolerated, the guardians of conciliar tradition and scripture, the patriarchs and under them the bishops, did not have much room for manoeuvre where a definition existed.[2]

On the other hand, the western bishops, and particularly their leaders the popes, felt themselves free to adopt a more flexible approach. Although as late as the eleventh century the early general councils had a special place in the thinking of Latin churchmen[3] – indeed in a sense they still have it – the fact that from the early twelfth century the popes began to call their own general councils tells us a great deal about the differences on the issue of authority that were emerging. The schism between Rome, representing Catholicism, and Constantinople, representing Orthodoxy, is often described solely in jurisdictional terms, with reference to the popes' conviction that they were the supreme governors of the church under Christ and could therefore judge other patriarchs and hear cases on appeal from within other patriarchates. But since the popes saw their primacy, including jurisdiction, in the light of functions which were considered to have been in the mind of Christ when he commissioned St Peter, their role as universal judges was a doctrinal matter.

Throughout the debates on the nature of Christ the popes had held pugnaciously to a particular line, in which they had had the general support of the western bishops. Some popes had succumbed to pressure from emperors in Constantinople intent on finding a form of words which would unite the opposing factions, but others, like Martin I who died in exile in the Crimea, had suffered for the stand they had made. The fact that in the end it was the beliefs about the nature of Christ for which they had fought that came to be held throughout Greek and Latin Christendom demonstrated to the popes themselves that they did indeed have a special and authoritative voice on matters of doctrine. That was why the issue of the procession of the Holy Spirit, the *filioque* clause, which from the ninth century onwards divided Greeks and Latins more than any other question, became so significant. The creed, or statement of belief, of the fourth-century councils of Nicaea and Constantinople [I], two of the authoritative seven, which had summarized the orthodox position on the Holy Spirit, had declared that the Holy Spirit 'proceeds from the father'. The addition of the phrase 'and the son (*filioque*)' first appeared in Spain in the late sixth century, gradually spread throughout the west and, in spite of an attempt to suppress it made by Pope Leo III early in the ninth century, was adopted in Rome soon after 1000.[4] In their apparent insouciance the popes, who by blithely altering the wording of one of the sacred conciliar decrees had ignored Greek attachment to them, were delivering the message that they could legitimize a change to dogma without reference to any other authority. Indeed, in later centuries strong pressure was put by them on the Greeks to adopt the change themselves.

It was Robert Bellarmine, the shrewdest of all apologists for Catholicism, who pointed out in the late sixteenth century that Christianity had been divided on two fundamental issues: first the nature of the Trinity and then the nature of the church itself.[5] The nature of the church was conditioned by its authority and already by the end of the first millennium the attitudes of the two halves of Christendom to this question were diverging sharply. In 1049 the papacy was seized by a group of radicals, so that for almost the only time in its history it was at the forefront of reform, and it is not surprising that in the fields of faith and morals there followed a period of extraordinarily rapid development. The transformation of the sacramental and penitential theology of the Catholic church, the geographical location of Purgatory and the establishment of universal rules for canonization and for the verification of relics were all matters that directly affected ordinary Christians. Proclaiming that it had an independent authoritative voice, alongside that of general councils and the consensus of the teaching of all the bishops, and reinforcing this with institutional controls, which were now achievable in an environment marked by economic and technological development, the spread of education and structural innovation, the papacy was able to loosen the chains of pre-existing doctrinal authority. It would be going too far to assert that it was now free-wheeling – indeed, it always assured anyone who would listen of its devotion to precedent, previous councils and scripture – but its pre-eminence and the respect with which its voice was generally heard meant that it could oversee adaptation and development. Between 1123 and 1312 it summoned no less than seven new general councils,[6] while the judgements streaming from the papal curia meant that the standard codification of canon law, Gratian's *Decretum* of *c.*1140, had to be regularly updated with supplementary works.[7] Catholic authority, therefore, was characterized by its ability to issue a succession of pronouncements on faith and morals, each claiming, of course, to be only expressing what had been in the mind of the church from the start. The Catholic church liked to portray itself as conservative, and still does, whereas in fact it represents arguably the most radical of all brands of Christianity. What other branch of the religion in the last century and a half would have dared to lay down as eternal truths the Immaculate Conception and Assumption of Our Lady and Papal Infallibility? This adaptability was only made possible by the existence of an autocracy at the centre, claiming the power to oversee the whole church on Christ's behalf and having the freedom that went with it.

Early in the second millennium, therefore, Greek and Latin Christendom, one doctrinally static if generally tolerant of anything not covered by authoritative conciliar pronouncement, the other doctrinally fluid but intolerant of anything deviating from its latest statement on faith, were drifting apart and the differences between them became unbridgeable when the West launched crusades which conquered the seats of the patriarchates of Antioch, Jerusalem and Constantinople and imposed Latin hierarchies against the wishes of the indigenous Greeks.[8] Half-way through the second millennium, however, the West itself was sundered in a Reformation which can be seen in part as a reaction to Catholic adaptability in an age when the emergence of Christian humanism promised even more radical change.

It was, needless to say, the issue of authority which divided the western church in the sixteenth century, when a group of clever theologians, pre-eminent among them Jean Calvin, took advantage of the fact that intellectual circles were arguing that it was in need of moral and institutional reform. As we know, classic Protestantism is marked by the belief that the only authentic authority is scripture and by a consequent denial of the intermediary role of the church. The authority of scripture is grounded partly on the fact that it is divinely inspired and partly on 'the internal testimony of the Holy Spirit', which can persuade the believer of its validity. Whereas in Orthodoxy scripture was interpreted in the light of the doctrinal decisions of the first seven councils and in Catholicism under the guidance of an authoritative teaching voice, in Protestantism the authentic authority for the interpretation of the Word was the Word itself. The faithful found themselves in a loop, in which the ambiguities in revelation could only be resolved through its own ambiguities. And while it was believed that the authority of scripture expressed itself not only objectively, but also subjectively in the response of the believer to it, there had to develop in practice collective interpretations which, in spite of the limited role accorded to corporate church structures – or at least a failure to agree about them – led communities to different forms – if often fairly autocratic forms – of self-governance. The dilemma faced by most Protestants was not as severe as it sounds, because some of the rulers who had adopted the new faith were anxious that it should encompass as many of their subjects as possible. So there soon emerged inclusive variants in which wide divergences in belief were tolerated, at the expense, it must be said, of coherence. Nevertheless, with the notion of self-authenticating scripture Protestantism had reintroduced a firm framework of belief, even if it was one that was at the same time so rigid and so debatable that adaptation could only be achieved through the formation of separate sects. It was this, I think, that made Protestantism so fissile, leading within a century to yet another divergence on authority with some groups, like the Quakers, subordinating scripture to the testimony of the Holy Spirit. One fairly common reaction of Protestants to their difficulties was to deny they existed. They maintained that scripture was not ambiguous at all and should be followed to the letter. Growing scientific understanding of the natural world in the nineteenth century, however, and the work of Protestant biblical scholars made a literal reading of scripture much harder to defend; indeed, for all

Protestants critical exegesis threatened the authority they recognized and some have turned in what looks very like despair to philosophy.

Curiously enough Christianity has continued to grow throughout the second millennium, mostly in the wake of European imperialism, with the faith following the occupation of America, Africa and parts of Asia. That 64 per cent of all Christians are Catholic and that there are more Anglicans in the world than Baptists are facts surely more dependent on Spanish, Portuguese and English conquest than on any intrinsic doctrinal merit. But at any rate growth has only exacerbated the differences. Christianity is now in a mess, even more fragmented than it was in 1000. The roots of that fragmentation – differing approaches to authority – were already forming themselves in the first millennium.

In the year 1000 Islam looked even more divided than Christianity. The Sunni majority was confronted by an aggressive, expanding Shi'ism, orchestrated from Cairo, from which was emanating brilliant propaganda.[9] Shi'ism had originated in the civil wars which had broken out after 'Ali, the Prophet's cousin and son-in-law, who had seized the caliphate, had been assassinated in 661 and his younger son, Husayn, who had led a revolt against the caliph Yazid, had been killed at Karbala in 680. Whereas for Sunni Muslims religious authority lies in the consensus of the community reflecting the holy law, the *shari'a*, which has been shaped by the *sunna*, a body of orally transmitted learned traditions relating to the words and deeds of the Prophet and his companions, Shi'ites believe that supreme religious authority was held by 'Ali and then by a line of imams who were his spiritual successors. One group of Shi'ites maintain that after the disappearance into supernatural occlusion of the twelfth imam in *c.* 873, spiritual authority is in abeyance until he should return. Another group, the Isma'ilis, hold to the authority of the seventh imam, who disappeared in 760. Imams in hiding are a feature of Shi'ism: occultation was later claimed for the Fatimid caliph Hakim, who mysteriously disappeared in the desert in 1021, and for his successors Nizar, who had been walled up in one of the great new gates of Cairo in 1094, and the child Tayyib, who had died mysteriously in 1130.[10] Whereas the Sunni 'Abbasid caliph in Baghdad had as his chief duty the enforcement rather than the authorization of the *shari'a*, the Fatimid caliph in

Cairo, who claimed descent from 'Ali and was believed to have inherited the powers of the seventh imam, both laid down the law and enforced it; according to a contemporary writer he was not only the authority for the open doctrine of Islam, but as the keeper of the word of God he was also the supreme authority for the hidden meaning of the Koran, being its only certain intellectual guide. Fatimid Shi'ism was fuelled by the belief that the caliphs had the mission of reviving the faith and Shi'ites were popping up everywhere, from India to the Maghreb; the Shi'ite Buyid dynasty in western Iran even controlled the 'Abbasid caliphate, although, being Twelvers, the Buyids did not recognize the Sevener Fatimids.[11]

The so-called 'Shi'ite century of Islam' ended in violent reaction, initiated by Sunni tribal groupings like the Seljuq Turks, who in the mid eleventh century had the zeal of recent converts to the faith, and the Fatimid dynasty was brought to an end in 1171, but Shi'ism as a major political force was to be revived with the conquest of Iran by the Twelver Safavids and the consolidation of their power there in the sixteenth century.[12]

Like Catholicism, Shi'ism, particularly in Iran, finds it relatively easy to innovate. Shi'a *ulama*, or learned men, came to be regarded as *mujtahids*, who had the right in the absence of the hidden imam to establish rulings in holy law in a way not open to Sunni teachers.[13] Even if one leaves aside the antipathy arising from the civil wars – the commemoration of Husayn's death at Karbala has become a defining feature of Shi'ism – and the periodic persecution of Shi'ites by Sunni states, it is hard to see how conservative and consensus-inspired Sunnism can be reconciled with charismatic and innovatory Shi'ism.

For most of the last millennium – and for centuries before the year 1000 – most Christians and Muslims have looked to violence to provide a solution to these internal divisions. It has been an unarguable conclusion to all but a tiny minority that in the last resort religious authority – whether expressed by councils and maintained by a hierarchy, or exercised by popes, or preached through scripture, or taught in the name of hidden imams or the consensus of the learned – can only be maintained by force. The majority opinion in Christianity was formed by theologians writing around 400, with respect particularly to what St Augustine of Hippo came to believe was a 'just persecution' of heretics. To Augustine it was right, and a sign of love and mercy in imitation of Christ, for a loving Church in collaboration with a loving state to force heretics from the path of error for their own benefit, compelling them to goodness in the same way as in Christ's parable the host at the feast had sent out his servant to *force* those on the highways to come to the banquet.[14] The features that made violence positive were, first, that it could be employed on behalf of Christ and could even be directly authorized by him; and, second, that it was a morally neutral force which drew whatever ethical colouring it had from the intentions of the perpetrators. It was only in the sixteenth century that Christ's authority for the use of force came to be replaced by the Aristotelian idea of 'the common good', the defence of which was the prerogative of every community. A catalyst appears to have been the atrocities committed by the Spaniards against the Indians in the New World and the critical reaction to them of the Dominican Francisco de Vitoria; in fact, the alternative title of *De Jure Belli*, his course of lectures in 1538–9, is *De Indiis Secunda*. For Vitoria and his followers, particularly Suarez and Ayala, the chief justification of violence was the common good, not any divine plan. With Ayala, indeed, just war arguments moved from the field of moral theology to that of law, a step developed within decades by Gentili and Grotius.[15] With the replacement of the idea of violence directly or indirectly authorized by God or Christ with that of violence for the common good, the justification of which had to be in accordance with accepted earthly laws, Christ had withdrawn from the fray, at least as far as Enlightenment thinkers were concerned: the *Encyclopédistes* referred to the crusades, the most characteristic of all wars for Christ, as 'ces guerres horribles'.[16] If you had asked most Enlightenment thinkers how they could justify war I think they would probably have replied that in some cases a foreseeable good – the common good – could outweigh a predictable evil, but one should stress that the evil they referred to was not violence itself but the suffering that accompanied it. Although there was general agreement that the use of force nearly always had evil consequences, violence itself was still regarded as being morally neutral, as it continued to be for Marxists. No one had yet taken the second step necessary for the emergence of modern just war theory, the borrowing from pacifism of the conviction that violence is intrinsically evil, accompanied by the argument that it can nevertheless be condoned as a lesser evil. I do not know when the crucial transference from pacifism into war-theory took place, but I suspect it was an achievement of the peace movement which swept Europe and America after the Napoleonic Wars and split into two wings, pacifist and moderate, in the 1830s.

It is astonishing how quickly the old ideas became forgotten. Modern just war theory – that violence, divorced from divine intentions, is not morally neutral but an evil which can in certain situations be condoned as the lesser of evils – has more or less held the field among respectable writers for only a century, a period unique in Christian history which requires explanation, and is anyway now in danger of being swept away, as the signs multiply that ideas of positive force are returning to the Christian scene. The old notion of violence for Christ, in which he is intimately involved, was certainly manifesting itself among Catholics in Latin America in the 1960s. Some North American Protestant bodies are justifying the arming of Christian minorities in Muslim states. A religious dimension cannot be denied in Northern Ireland, the Balkans, Lebanon and Indonesia, even if it is hard to decide whether in some instances religion is a cloak for nationalism. A secularized version is leading to the waging of wars justified by their 'humanitarian' aims. This last development, one should note, reverses the achievement of the sixteenth-century thinkers, demotes international law and reintroduces subjective ethical judgements to just war theory.

Many modern writers, assuming that a comparatively recent development is as old as the hills, continue to maintain that Christianity is fundamentally a religion of peace, whereas there are strong grounds for supposing that violence is embedded in it, as it is in Islam and possibly in all revealed religions. It is not easy to turn one's back on a catalogue of examples of the physical repression of religious deviance in the name of whatever authority the deviants are questioning: the Frankish campaigns against the Arian Visigoths in the sixth century, repressive measures against heretics throughout Christendom from the eleventh century, Catholic violence preached in Rome, Orthodox violence preached in Constantinople and Moscow, religious wars in western Europe in the sixteenth and seventeenth centuries, Catholic persecutors of Protestants, Protestant persecutors of Catholics, and polemicists on both sides in the English Civil War.

In Islam the *jihad* – a striving after perfection in self, the community and the world – was interpreted as a collective obligation to make war upon non-Muslims until they submitted to Muslim rule, whether as converts or as *dhimmis*, tolerated persons of certain recognized religions, including Judaism and Christianity. Between the *dar al-islam* (the Land of Islam) and the *dar al-harb* (the Land of War) there was a continual state of enmity, suspended temporarily by safe-conduct or truce, even if most Muslims for most of the time did not feel themselves obliged to be continuously at war with outsiders and some have interpreted *jihad* to mean an effort at interior self-development.[17]

Christianity and Islam were in conflict spasmodically from the seventh to the eighteenth centuries, confronting each other in wars which for Christians often became crusades. What is noteworthy is how these wars actually encouraged the introspective violence to which I have referred. Sacred violence can take several forms, of course, but the category of holy war to which crusading and the *jihad* belong – extraliminal in the sense that it is initially proclaimed against an external force – seems to have a tendency to turn inwards sooner or later and to be directed against the members of the very society which has generated it. As war takes hold the conviction grows that any chance of victory can be vitiated by corruption or divisions at home, so that only when society is undefiled and is practising uniformly true religion can the war on its behalf be successful. In the twelfth-century Near East, where a *jihad* was being waged against the crusaders, there was a movement, particularly under Nur ad-Din, the Muslim ruler of Damascus and Egypt, for moral rearmament, characterized by the suppression of heresies, particularly Shi'ism.[18] Further west, in the Maghreb and Spain, the Almohads, trying to stem the Christian advance, were not alone in distinguishing the greater *jihad*, involving ethical and spiritual renewal, from the lesser, which related to war. The climax of this movement came around 1300 with the remarkable and charismatic Ibn Taymiyya, for whom the priority of the *jihad* was at that stage not to wage war in the *dar al-harb*, but to purge the Sunni world of infidels and heretics. As far as Jews and Christians were concerned, Ibn Taymiyya argued that while the goal of Muslims must be the eventual eradication of their imperfect monotheism this should be achieved not by outright persecution, but by the strict application of the *dhimma* regulations. He condemned the Shi'ites as interior enemies 'even more dangerous than the Jews and the Christians' and he wanted holy war to be waged pitilessly against them. For him the *jihad* was a force which at the same time would renew individual spirituality and create a society dedicated to God which could then triumph over the world.[19] His lasting influence is demonstrated by the way the assassins of President Sadat of Egypt justified their act on the basis of his writings, and Sunnites have been fighting Shi'ites in Afghanistan and allegedly oppressing them in Iraq.

Much the same desire to cleanse the home front was being expressed in western Europe at a popular level from the moment the First Crusade was preached – it probably contributed to the persecution of the Jews in France and the Rhineland in 1096 – and it was officially adopted forty years later when Pope Innocent II presided over a council at Pisa which decreed that those who fought the pope's enemies – in this case the south Italian Normans and the anti-pope Anacletus – should enjoy the crusade remission of sins; it cannot be a coincidence that the polemics mouthed against the anti-pope dwelt on the fact that he had a Jewish grandfather. Some time later Peter the Venerable, the influential abbot of Cluny, was prepared to argue that violence against fellow-Christians could be more justifiable than the use of force against infidels; and the need to purify Christianity was being even more openly expressed following the disasters which overtook the Christian settlements in Palestine in 1187, including the loss of Jerusalem to Saladin. 'We should first', wrote Pope Gregory VIII, 'amend in ourselves what we have done wrong and then turn our attention to the treachery and malice of the enemy.' From the Fourth Lateran Council in the early thirteenth century to the Council of Trent in the middle of the sixteenth every general council of the Catholic church was officially summoned on the grounds that no crusade could be really successful without a reform of the church and of Christendom.

It is surely no coincidence, therefore, that the less successful crusades against external foes became the more regularly they were redirected internally. In the traumatic period that followed the loss of Jerusalem introspective crusades were often preached in the name of extraliminal war against Islam. Pope Innocent III accused the representative of Staufen interests in Italy, Markward of Anweiler, against whom he proclaimed a crusade in 1199, of threatening his preparations for a campaign in the east and when calling for a crusade against the heretical Cathars in 1208 – in propaganda replete with imagery of uncleanness and disease – he summoned the crusaders to launch themselves against heretics 'that much more confidently than you would attack the Muslims because they are worse than them'. Although this was obviously not the first occasion on which force had been used against the popes' political opponents or authorized against heretics – it was not even the first time war had been waged on them, as we have seen – the redirection against enemies within Christendom of an army of crusaders involved pressurizing men who had taken the cross to confront an external foe in the east to commute their vows in favour of internal police actions.[20]

But in the end all this violence led nowhere, partly because in Christianity force could only be perpetrated by laymen and by secular powers acting in support of the church and some of those powers themselves came to adhere to deviant faith and used violence to defend their own cause. The same was true in Islam, where the conversion of Iran to Shi'ism provided it with a strong base. So Shi'ism remains a force in Islam and the differences in Christianity are as strong as ever, if not stronger, because they are fuelled by memories of past inter-confessional violence. Although in this century the ecumenical movement has led Christians – or some of them – to be more polite to one another and even to take joint initiatives, it has come no nearer to providing a solution. I am inclined to think that most ecumenists do not recognize how basic the differences are. It is no good referring solely to scripture when debating with bodies who revere it but do not believe it can be self-authenticating. It is no good drawing attention to 'tradition' – a euphemism if ever there was one – when in discussion with those who believe in a more inflexible basis of authority. It is no good criticizing authoritarian forms of church government in the presence of churchmen whose confession is dependent on them. In this respect the last millennium has built on the first only in the sense that in both religions it has aggravated fundamental differences that already existed.

Notes and References

1 A.T. Welch, 'al-Ku'ran', *The Encyclopedia of Islam*, new edn, vol. 5 (Leiden, 1986), cols 402, 403.

2 For medieval Orthodoxy, see J.M. Hussey, *The Orthodox Church in the Byzantine Empire* (Oxford, 1986), *passim*.

3 See H.E.J. Cowdrey, *Pope Gregory VII* (Oxford, 1998), pp. 406, 517.

4 J.N.D. Kelly, *Early Christian Creeds*, 3rd edn (Harlow, 1972), pp. 358–67.

5 See J. Brodrick, *Robert Bellarmine, Saint and Scholar* (London, 1961), pp. 53–4.

6 For the Catholic definition of councils, see *Dictionnaire de droit canonique*, ed. R. Naz, vol. 3 (Paris, 1942), cols 1280–301.

7 See J.A. Brundage, *Medieval Canon Law* (London, 1995), pp. 44–70.

8 J.S.C. Riley-Smith, *The Crusades: A Short History* (London, 1987), *passim*.

9 See M. Brett, 'The Near East on the Eve of the Crusades', *La Primera Cruzada Novecientos Años Después: el Concilio de Clermont y los Origenes del Movimiento Cruzado*, ed. L. García-Guijarro Ramos (Madrid, 1997), pp. 124–34.

10 R. Irwin, 'Islam and the Crusades', *The Oxford Illustrated History of the Crusades*, ed. J.S.C. Riley-Smith (Oxford, 1995), pp. 218–19; S.M. Stern, 'The Succession to the Fatimid Imam al-Amir, the Claims of the Later Fatimids to the Imamate, and the Rise of Tayyibi Ismailism', *Oriens* 4 (1951), pp. 193–255; W. Madelung, 'Imama', *The Encylopedia of Islam*, vol. 3 (Leiden, 1971), cols 1166–9; W. Madelung, 'Shi'a', *ibid.* vol. 9 (Leiden, 1997), cols 420–4; G.H.A. Juynboll, 'Sunna', *ibid.*, cols 878–81.

11 M. Brett, 'Abbasids, Fatimids and Seljuqs', *The New Cambridge Medieval History*, vol. 4.2, ed. J.S.C. Riley-Smith (Cambridge, forthcoming).

12 *The Cambridge History of Islam*, ed. P.M. Holt, A.K.S. Lambton and B. Lewis, vol. 1 (Cambridge, 1970), pp. 398–9.

13 F. Robinson, *Atlas of the Islamic World since 1500* (Oxford, 1982), p. 47.

14 See J.S.C. Riley-Smith, 'Crusading as an act of love', *History* 65 (1980), pp. 185–7; F.H. Russell, *The Just War in the Middle Ages* (Cambridge, 1975), pp. 16–26.

15 H. Duchhardt, 'La guerre et le droit des gens dans l'Europe du XVIe au XVIIIe siècle', *Guerre et concurrence entre les Etats européens du XIVe au XVIIIe siècle*, ed. P. Contamine (Paris, 1998), pp. 344–56.

16 D. Diderot and J. Le R. d'Alembert, *Encyclopédie*, vol. 4 (Paris, 1754), p. 505.

17 A. Morabia, *Le Gihad dans l'Islam médiéval* (Paris, 1983), *passim*.

18 E. Sivan, *L'Islam et la croisade* (Paris, 1968), pp. 70–2.

19 A. Morabia, 'Ibn Taymiyya, dernier grand théoricien du Gihad médiéval',

Bulletin d'études orientales, 30 (1978), pp. 85–99; C. Hillenbrand, *The Crusades: Islamic Perspectives* (Edinburgh, 1999), pp. 241–3.

20 J.S.C. Riley-Smith, 'Christian Violence and the Crusades', *Religious Violence between Christians and Jews*, ed. A. Sapir Abulafia (Basingstoke, 2002), pp. 3–20.

ROSAMOND MCKITTERICK

Europe and the Carolingian Inheritance

To mark the opening of the exhibition *799 Kunst und Kultur der Karolingerzeit* (799: Carolingian Art and Culture), on 23 July 1999, an elaborate three-hour ceremony was conducted in Paderborn's tenth-century cathedral (itself an enlargement of the original late eighth-century building). The first of many speeches was given by the then *Bundespräsident* Johannes Rau. He recalled how the leaders of G-7, now the G-8, states had met in Cologne shortly beforehand, and that they had not realized that the first European summit meeting had taken place 1200 years earlier, also in territory now in present-day Germany, not on the Rhine but in Nordrhein-Westfalen. The meeting was between Charles, king of the Franks, and Pope Leo III and was what Rau described as a 'G-2 summit': 'Denn es waren die beiden westlichen Großmächte, die weltliche und die geistliche, die sich im Jahre 799 hier trafen.' (It was the two Western superpowers of the day, the secular and the spiritual, who met here in 799.)[1]

Rau was referring to the meeting at Paderborn recorded in contemporary Frankish narrative sources as well as in an epic poem written at the beginning of the ninth century known as the *Paderborn Epic* or *Carolus magnus et Leo papa*.[2] The narrative sources, such as the Royal Frankish Annals and the 'Lorsch' annals, recount the problems in Rome encountered by the new Pope, Leo III, who had succeeded Pope Hadrian I in 796. Faction fighting in Rome had culminated in a savage attack on Pope Leo himself. Pope Leo came to Paderborn, where the king was residing in a newly-built palace next to the equally

new cathedral. Leo appears to have succeeded in winning Charlemagne's support, an escort back to Rome and assistance in dealing
with his enemies there.[3]

The *Paderborn Epic* commemorates the meeting at Paderborn in
Latin of Virgilian tone, vocabulary and borrowed imagery. The poem
is crammed full of extravagant praise for the Frankish king, Charles.
The poet, having finished two long sections of the poem, describes
how:

> The gusts of the mild east wind swiftly shake and fill the sails
> rapidly driving me on to the hard course before me,
> to where the beacon of Europe [*pharus Europae*] gleams with light from
> afar.
> Charlemagne's outstanding name is broadcast to the stars.[4]

The meeting of the king and the pope itself is described at length and
adorned with rousing speeches. Again reference is made to Europe –
the king who is father of Europe, *pater Europae*, and Leo, the 'world's
highest pastor', walk together and exchange views.[5]

I shall leave aside, for the moment, the Paderborn exhibition itself,
the *Bundespräsident*'s theatrical, political analogy to a 'G-2 summit'
and his highlighting, in the next portion of his speech, of the
coronation of Charlemagne as emperor in Rome on Christmas Day
800. I shall instead concentrate on the idea, expressed 1200 years ago,
of Charlemagne as the father of Europe.

The idea of Europe itself, of course, was expressed by the Greeks.
Herodotus referred to the world as divided into Europe, Asia and
Libya.[6] Many subsequent authors – Ephonis, Eratosthenes, Strabo,
Ptolemy and Agrippa, discuss the division of the world. Much ancient
knowledge, indeed, is summed up by Dicuil, an Irish geographer at
the court of Charlemagne, who thought Agrippa was the first to divide
the world into Europe, Asia and Africa: 'The earth is divided into
three sections, namely, Europe, Asia and Libya and this the deified
Augustus was first to exhibit by means of his world map. All my work
takes its beginning then from the strait of Europe, which place the
Greeks name the columns of Hercules.'[7]

In ninth-century representations of the world, often incorporated
into the popular and widely available encyclopaedic work of Isidore of

Seville known as the *Etymologiae*, this threefold division of the sphere of the earth is represented in a graphically simple way in the form known as the TO map.[8] Europe as a territorial concept in the eighth and ninth centuries, therefore, is part of an ancient understanding of the division of the world, but the *Paderborn Epic* seems to be using it in a political sense as well: Europe for this poet is the area over which Charlemagne ruled. It is this, and its implications, namely the formation of Europe and the deep roots of the political and cultural understanding of Europe, that are among the concerns of this volume. The antique allusions in the *Paderborn Epic* are deliberate, of course, but we need to look in this chapter at the practical dimension to the claims made by the poet that Charlemagne was both the 'lighthouse' and the 'father' of Europe. That is, what was the physical and territorial extent of Charlemagne's empire? What were the political, religious and cultural consequences of the Frankish expansion over so vast a territory? Lastly, what was the ideological legacy of Charlemagne's empire?

The responses to these three questions will provide some indication of Europe's Carolingian inheritance.

The Physical and Territorial Extent of the Carolingian Empire

Let us look first, briefly, at the extraordinary expansion of the territory ruled by Charlemagne. Essentially he expanded the borders of the Frankish realm far beyond the areas controlled by his predecessors, the Merovingian kings of the Franks, even in their heyday, and even beyond the areas incorporated into the provinces of the former western Romen empire.

Charlemagne's grandfather Charles Martel had been the *de facto* ruler of the then northern part of the Frankish kingdom. He occupied a position known as the mayor of the palace, or 'prime minister', and even ruled on his own, without elevating another member of the Merovingian family to the kingship, for the last four years of his life, 737–41.[9] Charles Martel, in his turn, had consolidated the efforts made by his father, the mayor of the palace, Pippin II, to extend Merovingian territory into southern Frisia as well as to reconstitute the former Merovingian kingdoms. Charles Martel's own work was continued after 741 by his son Pippin III, who conquered Alemannia and Aquitaine and in 751 usurped the kingship itself. His succession was distinguished by the introduction of a new ritual, the anointing of the king at his coronation. The rituals and prayers subsequently devised by the Frankish clergy, most notably those of Archbishop Hincmar of Rheims (d. 882), formed the basis of those adopted in Anglo-Saxon England and used thereafter, even for the coronation of Queen Elizabeth II in 1953.[10]

As the next in a remarkable succession of able warriors and administrators, Pippin III's son Charlemagne then embarked on an extraordinarily ambitious series of conquests and annexations. A political coup established Charlemagne as the ruler of the Lombard kingdom of Italy in 774; Bavaria was annexed in 788; Saxony, after thirty years of savage military campaigning, was finally subdued in 798; the Avars were defeated in 796 (a success which brought great material wealth to the Franks); the Franks extended into the Spanish March in 795 and into Brittany by 812. Charlemagne and his son Pippin of Italy exercised a considerable amount of political influence in Dalmatia and Croatia in the early years of the ninth century. The conquest of the Saxons as well as Pippin II's and Charles Martel's earlier pushes northwards into Frisia had also brought the Franks into contact, potential conflict and certainly economic competition, especially in the North Sea and the Baltic, with the Danes, with whom there was a flurry of diplomatic arrangements and, thereafter, skirmishes which became increasingly aggressive in nature.[11]

As far as the Pope in Rome was concerned, Pippin III had been acknowledged as a protector of the papacy from 754 and accorded the title of patrician. Charlemagne inherited the close relationship with the pope. It was particularly close and respectful between Charlemagne and Hadrian. Between Charlemagne and Leo III, however, it was more a relationship between protector and grateful dependant respectively, which culminated in Charlemagne being crowned as emperor of the Romans in 800. In Charlemagne's own reign the ideological implications of this event remained undeveloped. Arrangements he made in 806 for the succession made no reference to the imperial title and split his empire between his then three legitimate sons. But by 813 Charlemagne was induced to pass on to his sole surviving son, Louis (the Pious), both the title and the entire empire and it was in Louis's reign that a specifically imperial ideology began to be elaborated.

The Political, Religious and Cultural Consequences of Empire

The political, religious and cultural consequences of this astonishing expansion of the Frankish realm, from an area roughly equivalent to present-day France to one embracing most of present-day Western Europe, from the northern Netherlands to central Italy and from Brittany to eastern Austria, were manifold. Administrative structures, law, religion and culture together helped to consolidate the empire as a coherent polity.

Although the Carolingians created a new focus of power in Austrasia – the Frankish kingdom in the north-east region stretching from the Champagne over the Meuse and Moselle to the Rhine rivers – centred on Cologne, Aachen, Liège, Nijmegen and the Mosan region, new centres also became prominent. For instance, there were new palaces built at Frankfurt, Ingelheim and Paderborn to supplement Merovingian, Bavarian and Lombard residences continuing in use, such as Soissons, Paris, Chelles, Compiègne and Berny (near Soissons), Regensburg and Pavia.[12] Paris was eclipsed under Charlemagne and his immediate successors. Rural palaces such as Attigny, Ponthion, Herstal, Aachen and Thionville were the administrative residences as well as the hunting lodges of an essentially itinerant king. There was never a capital city or chief city to compare with Toledo under the Visigothic rulers of Spain, or Pavia under the Lombard kings of Italy in the seventh and eighth centuries, though the palace complex created at Aachen in the latter years of the eighth century was of lasting importance and symbolic resonance.[13]

Royal residences and estates can be seen as one expression of royal power. Aachen may well represent an attempt to establish a centre for the Carolingian empire and was certainly a resplendent statement of royal wealth and status. But one essential accompaniment of the palaces as royal residences was the royal estate or fisc. The fiscal lands of the Frankish kings were concentrated between the Loire and

Scheldt rivers. Palaces were generally sited with various facilities in mind: strategy, communications, main routes (sea, river, road), lands of the loyal fisc for supplies and forests for hunting.

The energy put into administration and justice by the king himself was also emulated by the officials installed in the localities and the elaborate system of counties and *missatica* (administrative districts) regularly inspected by the king's agents known as the *missi dominici*. There was a restructuring of the royal household; the writing office was reorganized with the office of chaplain (head of the palace chapel) becoming increasingly prominent and the *cancellarii* or notaries of the royal writing office presiding for many years over the redaction of royal diplomas. The charters and other documents emanating from the royal writing office not only reflect the continuity of many basically Roman forms of documentary practice, but also provided the underlying model for the subsequent forms of royal and local legal records and organization of royal administration and protocol in the Middle Ages.[14] Law was emphasized and a wide variety of law books produced. Writing and written communication played a crucial role in administering this vast empire. The use of the written word, especially in religious matters and in legal transactions, permeated down through every level of society, even if the more elaborate and learned manifestations of intellectual activity were confined to an elite.[15]

Charlemagne was first and foremost a Christian ruler. The Frankish realm became coterminous with western Christendom in the determined spread of Christianity and Frankish Christian culture in the Carolingian period. Many new bishoprics were founded, at Paderborn, Münster, Bremen, Minden, Halberstadt, Hildesheim and Osnabrück, and a network of new monasteries was established, especially in Saxony. In the course of the savage wars of conquest, Charlemagne had forced Christianity upon the Saxons. The bishoprics and monasteries were the institutional strongholds from which clergy were sent out to consolidate Christian teaching, and to which the conquered peoples were increasingly recruited, as indeed they were into the army and administration, whether local or central. Elsewhere Christianity was strengthened and consolidated; in other annexed areas which were already Christian when taken over by the Franks, Carolingian nominees were placed in abbacies and bishoprics.

A programme of religious reform was embarked upon in the middle of the eighth century. Some of the impetus for this was provided by the zealous English missionary Boniface, who became bishop of Mainz and worked with Pippin III's brother Carloman. Pippin III and his main ecclesiastical adviser, Chrodegang of Metz, swiftly followed suit. Reforming ideals and specific statements about discipline, orthodox faith and religious practice were issued as statements by the ruler or proclaimed at many of the assemblies presided over by the king and his lay and religious advisers in the later eighth and early ninth centuries, most notably the *Admonitio Generalis* of 789, the Synod of Frankfurt in 794 and the reform councils of 813. Enormous stress was placed on correct texts, proper conduct, rigorous discipline and tidy organization.[16]

Along with the Christian faith came the use of the Latin language, similarly introduced, where it was not already established, for purposes of government, law, education and religion across the entire realm. In the Frankish regions west of the Rhine, which emerged as the kingdom of France in due course, Latin was effectively the native language and evolved in the course of the ninth and tenth centuries into the Romance form which subsequently became French. Similarly, in Italy and northern Spain, Latin prevailed at all levels, only gradually developing into Italian, Catalan and Spanish in the late Carolingian period.[17] Even in the regions east of the Rhine, although forms of Old High German and Old Saxon constituted the vernacular, Latin was the principal official language and exerted a strong influence on the written forms of early German.[18] Thus the great abundance of written material surviving from this period is in Latin. Texts include laws, letters, treatises, histories, poetry, practical manuals on war, architecture and agriculture, legal documents, records of assemblies, liturgical and biblical books. There are also the works received from antiquity, and preserved in new copies. Carolingian writers contributed new works on theology, philosophy, law, history, geography, astronomy, music, medicine, cosmography, grammar, orthography, baptism, the mass and many more. The orthography and structure of the Latin used in Carolingian texts, moreover, were deliberately made to conform more strictly to old classical and Ciceronian standards than the Latin of the seventh and eighth centuries had done.

This, and the production of texts as well as the education of the new generation of young scholars, was achieved by means of the establishment of the Frankish intellectual and cultural traditions in centres, old and new, throughout the empire. It is this concentration of intellectual and cultural activity which is generally labelled the Carolingian Renaissance.[19] Charlemagne himself played a key role in giving it impetus.

The *Admonitio generalis* of 789, for example, issued by Charlemagne, in addition to its statements about the organization of the church and religious practice, had identified a need to correct the texts used for the Catholic religion. Chapter 72 decreed that 'schools for teaching boys the psalms, musical notation, singing, computation and grammar be created in every monastery and episcopal residence. And correct catholic books properly, for often, while people want to pray to God in the proper fashion, they yet pray improperly because of uncorrected books.'[20]

Both the *Admonitio generalis* of 789 and a later directive, the *De litteris colendis*, issued *c*. 800, also placed great emphasis on schools and education. The latter stressed that bishoprics and monasteries should not only devote themselves to the practice of the religious life and the observance of monastic discipline, but should also cultivate learning and educate the monks and secular clergy so that they might achieve a better understanding of the Christian writings.[21]

The text of the Bible itself was corrected and edited in the early Carolingian period.[22] Authoritative versions of other books for use in the churches and monasteries, such as the liturgical books for the mass, the Homilary or 'Book of sermons', the Antiphonary, canon law, and the Rule of Benedict, were also prepared. The aim was to establish uniform religious observance throughout the empire and copies of the approved and authorized versions of liturgical and ecclesiastical texts were widely disseminated. Some centres specialized in the production of particular categories of these books. Tours, for example, became famous for its magnificent large-format one-volume Bibles. These efforts to promote a standard religious observance created harmony rather than uniformity; yet diverse as practice remained, it was a distinctively Frankish diversity in that the texts deployed were those compiled by Franks and used in different parts of the Frankish realms for many years.

The requirements for correct texts and the emphasis on education within the great ecclesiastical centres meant that in the *scriptoria* (writing centres) of the Carolingian realm overall there was a prodigious output of books in comparison with the Merovingian period. These books served not only the needs of religious worship but also government and administration, spiritual discipline, intellectual endeavour, education and literary activity. In response to the need for texts, the distinctive Caroline minuscule that had evolved during the Merovingian period, based on Roman uncial, half uncial and cursive letter forms, was refined and disseminated throughout the empire and in due course introduced into Italy, England and Spain. Some centres simply acquired books from other *scriptoria* but most copied and created their own. Even the royal court had groups of scribes and artists associated with it.[23] The work of two groups of scribes and artists is attributed to the 'court school' of Charlemagne, producing art in very different styles from each other and writing the texts in uncial and the new caroline minuscule.

A crucial role in the religious, cultural and political life of the Frankish realm in the late eighth century was played by the versatile scholars from many countries congregated at the royal court and enjoying Charlemagne's patronage. These included the Franks Angilram, Wigbod, Einhard and Angilbert; Alcuin the Englishman from York; Theodulf, a Visigoth from Septimania; Paul the Deacon, Paulinus of Aquileia and Peter of Pisa from the Lombard kingdom; Joseph, Dicuil and Dungal from Ireland, and many more. The court coterie is depicted in many of the poems written by these creative scholars. Their intellectual interests embraced Christian theology as well as the metrical forms of classical antiquity. Major works such as the *Libri carolini* by Theodulf of Orleans on the place of art in the Christian church and the issue of iconoclasm, or the varied responses to the Spanish heresy of Adoptionism, are the direct outcome of the intense theological and philosophical discussion at court which involved the king himself. Many of the court scholars subsequently joined or set up monastic and cathedral schools and taught throughout the realm. Among these Alcuin taught at Tours (having first acted as personal tutor to Charlemagne and his daughters) and numbered many leading scholars of the next generation among his pupils, not least Hraban Maur of Fulda. He also continued his theological and pastoral discussions with Charlemagne's daughters, by then established at the convent of Chelles, in a series of a letters and biblical commentaries. Yet the scholars were often active administrators, and served the king and the empire as counts, bishops and abbots.

The Franks appear to have been very conscious of their role in preserving their Roman heritage and moulding it for their own purposes. One crucial aspect of ninth-century culture, indeed, is the formation of a canon of knowledge, reflected above all in the extant library catalogues of that century.[24] The bulk of the surviving manuscripts dating from before 800 and of the ninth century are in fact those of patristic, biblical and liturgical books, with Augustine, Jerome and Gregory the Great predominating among the patristic authors, and an increasing number of early medieval English, Italian and Frankish authors being introduced. But these patristic and early medieval works are of no less importance as far as the formation of European culture and the Carolingian *renovatio* are concerned. For one thing, the patristic authors were themselves well versed in the classics and passed on many of their cultural assumptions and allusions to succeeding generations. For another, their work in itself formed Christian life and thought. It is of the utmost importance to appreciate not only what the Carolingians revived and passed on, but also their own achievements. Carolingian scholars wrote learned commentaries on the Bible, treatises on grammar, spelling, philosophy, rhetoric, poetry and theological doctrine. Classical, patristic and Carolingian scholarship proved an enduring legacy within the European intellectual tradition. Many aspects of the curriculum, which became the *artes* of the medieval universities, had been developed in the late eighth and the ninth centuries.

Einhard, the first biographer of Charlemagne, writing in about 817, tells us that Charlemagne was taught many different subjects by Alcuin, that the king was very interested in music and what was being sung in his chapel, and that he liked to listen to the reading of stories and tales of the deeds of the ancient, or some other entertainment while dining.[25] The capitularies and conciliar decrees, not least those of the Synod of Frankfurt in 794 or the reform councils of 813, make clear how personal a part the king took in theological discussion and the reform of the clergy, ecclesiastical organization and the liturgy. In whatever resplendent new palace it was temporarily based (at Frankfurt, Paderborn or Aachen) as the king moved on the royal itinerary round the kingdom, the central role of the court as a place where scholars could congregate is indicative of the crucial role of the ruler as a patron of culture. When we observe other powerful early medieval polities where the kings did not play such a role, our appreciation of the Carolingian rulers' achievements and intellectual energy is greatly enhanced. The Carolingian ruler sustained groups of artists, scribes and craftsmen over a long period of time in order to create artefacts for his particular objectives. His patronage was designed to promote his royal power as a Christian king and to consolidate the Christian faith by disseminating the key texts on which that faith was based.

It is becoming clear, as historians re-examine the narrative sources, how the Franks themselves promoted a Frankish identity and image. There is a strong triumphalist message transmitted in Frankish historical writing. This message was continued well into the late ninth century by both contemporary authors such as Notker Balbulus and subsequently by modern historians.[26]

The Carolingian Legacy

The welding together of the Frankish Carolingian empire and creation of a strong educational and cultural tradition are easy to document. The enduringness of the inheritance has sometimes, at least in modern historiography, been underplayed.[27] Was the Carolingian achievement really ephemeral and all swept away as Suger, the twelfth-century abbot of St Denis, and his contemporaries swept away the Carolingian churches of France and replaced them with Gothic cathedrals?[28] How much endured? How much can be established as essential foundations for what followed? Are there real continuities or massive changes? As always with such historical questions, it is a case of both.[29]

One might point to the coinage. The idea of a single European currency, valid throughout the vast empire of the Franks under Charlemagne and his son, Louis the Pious, was lost, and is being fought out today against all kinds of irrelevant emotions. But what was not lost was the fiscal and commercial roles of money and the necessity for political control over it. By the end of the twelfth century, most of Europe had some form of regulated currency system.[30]

The new silver penny of a new weight had been introduced into Francia and subsequently England (closely connected by trade with Francia) towards the end of the seventh century. The silver penny replaced what had become an increasingly debased gold coinage that had been part of the monetary system of antiquity. The silver penny became the standard currency unit in medieval Europe. It had fiscal and commercial roles and was controlled tightly by the ruler. These early pennies were struck to a weight of 1.3 grams in both Francia and England. Pippin III, Charlemagne's father, made a radical innovation for Francia in 754 by identifying the royal authority under which the coins were produced and also (usually) the name of the mint; and the coins were made from flans cut out of thin metal sheeting (on the same principle as milk-bottle tops). Some 22 solidi or 264 pennies were minted from a pound of silver to provide 240 pennies to a solidus in circulation. Charlemagne extended the Carolingian penny or denarius to Lombard Italy in about 781, and papal coinage took the Frankish coin as its model.

With the major currency reforms of 794, the weight of the Carolingian penny was increased to 1.7 grams and there was a very considerable standardization of design. Anglo-Saxon coinage reforms paralleled those of the Franks but their weight standard, determined late in the reign of Offa of Mercia, was different at 1.4 grams, whereas before that English coins had been the same weight as the Frankish.

In 812 a new type of Frankish coin was minted bearing the portrait bust of Charlemagne on the obverse and this type was continued under Charlemagne's son and successor Louis the Pious. Louis instituted major recoinages in 818 and 822/3 but coins of 1.7 grams remained in circulation until *c.* 864. The so-called *Christiana religio* coins were minted throughout the empire until 840. It was an astonishing uniformity and freedom of circulation. Thus a single European currency operated in Europe for nearly a century, though the unified system was at its strongest under Louis the Pious. In Louis' reign foreign coinage was effectively excluded from the empire, new coins were minted throughout the empire to a single design and demonetized issues were swiftly removed from circulation. The weight was maintained and the silver content was high. Even Venice, within the Byzantine orbit, produced Louis' *Christiana religio* coinage in order to facilitate trade.[31]

I have already referred above to the elements of Carolingian culture and governmental methods. These provided the essential foundations for later medieval developments. It is striking that the learned writers of the eleventh and twelfth centuries, for example, were quite clear in their minds about their intellectual inheritance from the Carolingian period.[32] The legal records of the central and later Middle Ages can clearly be seen to have developed from the documents in the Carolingian period in format, formulae used, script, seals and other methods of authentification and the personnel responsible for their production. Or, if one considers the ecclesiastical landscape and division into dioceses, much of the Carolingian organization of territorial jurisdiction remained, just as the principal towns of the Franks remain important centres now. There is no shortage of evidence to support the claims of the Franks to have contributed so substantially to the foundations of Europe. In the establishment of an intellectual and educational tradition, the Carolingians laid down the framework for study in the schools and universities of the later medieval and early modern periods. The Franks were extraordinarily creative artists and musicians, and it was in the Carolingian period that musical notation (in the form of neumes) was first devised. The innovations they made in historical writing were emulated all over Europe thereafter. Even their script, Caroline minuscule, was adopted and slightly modified in the fifteenth century and forms the basis of the 'Roman' typeface we all still read today. In the urgency with which they supported and promoted the Christian faith and brought vast new territories into both the Frankish world and Christendom, they consolidated a common Christian culture right across Europe.

We need also, however, to address the impact on ideology and imagination. In terms of the reverence subsequently accorded Charlemagne, it is salutary to remember that a liturgical feast in honour of St Charlemagne was actually instituted in 1165 when Pope Alexander III canonized him and a cult of Charlemagne spread across Western Europe.[33] In literature, too, Charlemagne was presented in many different guises, but always as a valiant Christian warrior, in any number of medieval Latin and vernacular epics, such as the Old French *Chanson de Roland*, the Irish *Gabáltas searluis móir* and the

German *Kaiserchronik*.[34] The Carolingian emperors, most particularly Charlemagne but increasingly as a sort of composite super-emperor, moreover, provided political ideologues with a powerful model. This was not just a matter of claiming ancient descent, though that happened too, as Robert Peril's genealogies of the emperors of Austria descended from Charlemagne, published in French, Spanish, Latin and Dutch versions, illustrates.[35] Nor was it only an imperial ideal and its resonance with the Roman empire, though that proved one of the most powerful throughout the Middle Ages and into the early modern period, as Dürer's famous portrait and Cointin's *Charlemagne et le retablissement de l'empire roman*, published in 1666, indicate.[36] Charlemagne came to symbolize the common roots of European political and legal culture as much as the Carolingian scholars had established the basis of European religious, intellectual and visual culture. The extraordinary circumstances surrounding Charlemagne's tomb, for example, link the German emperor Otto III (d. 1002) and Napoleon.

In the cathedral treasury at Aachen is a spectacular sarcophagus, 2.15 metres long, 0.62 metres high and .64 metres broad, made of Carrara marble in the third century AD and carved with bas-relief sculture depicting the Rape of Prosperina. Einhard's *Vita Karoli* describes Charlemagne's death and his burial in the palace chapel at Aachen,[37] but we have nothing more precise about his tomb. The German historian of the eleventh century, Thietmar of Merseberg (d. 1018), describes how Otto III had Charlemagne disinterred and how his body was in a *solium* and uncorrupted.[38] The word *solium* presents considerable difficulties: it can mean 'shrine' or 'reliquary' or even 'bath' but it can also be used figuratively to mean 'dignity'. Thus Thietmar could be referring to the sarcophagus. Certainly, it has been regarded as Charlemagne's original resting place until 1165 when the Emperor Frederick Barbarossa had the body exhumed again and transferred to a gaudy new gold bust reliquary. The sarcophagus remained in Aachen until Napoleon took it to Paris but it was returned to Aachen in 1815. From 1843 to 1979, the public was no longer permitted to see it but in 1998 it was restored to its original glory for the Paderborn exhibition.[39] Napoleon's appropriation of this imperial sarcophagus was not just war booty. He regarded himself as the new Charlemagne.

Both Charlemagne and Napoleon were described by the author in the preface to the study of Charlemagne published in Brussels in 1848 as veritable demi-gods who, like Alexander the Great and other ancient conquering heroes, changed the course of history. The illustrator to this book also linked the imperial crown of Germany to Charlemagne. The frontispiece of *Charlemagne* (1848) anachronistically depicts Charlemagne being crowned by the pope with Otto's crown. The crown was probably made in the tenth century for Otto II, and remained part of the regalia of the Habsburg rulers thereafter (it was used, for example, for the coronation of the emperor Franz-Joseph II).[40] It is well known from Napoleon's letters to the Pope that Napoleon regarded Charlemagne as his illustrious predecessor.

What could be described as the nineteenth-century public imagination concerning Charlemagne's place in the history of Europe was reflected in the world of scholarship as well, where the period of the early Middle Ages was rightly recognized as formative for European culture. When in 1819, for example, the Monumenta Germaniae Historica (MGH) was founded to publish texts relating to the history of Germany in the Middle Ages, it is highly significant that the perception of what was relevant to the earlier history of Germany embraced authors from seventh- and eighth-century England such as Aldhelm and Bede, the Italian writer Cassiodorus, the Visigothic kings' laws, the writings of Gallo-Romans and Franks, the great band of writers who charted the activities of Irish, Frankish, Aquitainian, English and Frisian missionary saints and the poetry of Carolingian scholars, to mention only a handful of the great abundance of texts produced, and still being produced, in scholarly editions by this remarkable institution.[41] The spirit of the MGH's enterprise, echoed on rather more parochial scales in France, England and Italy, endures. A recent manifestation of European-wide collaboration in the study of Europe's past is the recently completed European Science Foundation's five-year project on *The Transformation of the Roman World and Emergence of Early Medieval Europe*. Over one hundred scholars from all the countries of the European Union, including many from Britain, were involved.[42]

That Charlemagne himself remains a symbol of European unity is clear from the existence of the *Prix Charlemagne*, instituted in 1953 and awarded to those promoting the cause of European unity. Our own Prime Minister, Tony Blair, was so honoured, perhaps a little prematurely, soon after taking up his first term of office. A similar post-war promotion of unity centred on Charlemagne was the comprehensive Council of Europe exhibition at Aachen in 1965 devoted to the Frankish emperor. The idea for this great display was born in the early 1950s as one possible means of rewelding Europeans together by emphasizing their shared past and common culture. Certainly the cultural inheritance of Europe as a whole has remained a strong theme among many international enterprises and celebratory conferences and exhibitions since then, not least the Paderborn exhibition commemorating 799 with which I began. Since the Second World War, it is perhaps more the cultural than the political legacy that has been stressed, but, nevertheless, the political and ideological resonances endure. Comparisons between the extent of territory included in Charlemagne's empire, Napoleon's Europe and modern Europe emphasize the underlying territorial and cultural continuities, however much the detailed political configurations may have altered since 843.[43]

Thus it is arguable that the claim of each European nation to a portion of the Carolingian inheritance might override the European element of his rule and the fact that the Carolingian empire stretched right across modern national boundaries. That is, studies of Carolingian France, Carolingian Germany or Carolingian Italy, for example, might focus too greatly on matters concerning only those areas within the modern territorial limits of these countries.[44] In this respect, European unity may be an inappropriate goal, but what we can achieve is harmony and an appreciation of rich diversity. Underlying the diversity of Europe should be, nevertheless, a deeper sense of a shared culture, not only of the Roman past but also of the Carolingian empire.

I return to Paderborn in 1999. From all over the world, scholars contributed to the catalogue and the accompanying volume of essays. The artefacts and books there, now in museums and libraries all over the world, were brought to northern Germany, and over 300,000 people visited this spectacular celebration of the Carolingian achievement. Whatever spin the *Bundespräsident* might have wished to put on it, the significance of Charlemagne's reign cannot and should not be ignored. It is for historians to determine what is achievement and what is ideological inheritance in order to prevent distortions of either being exploited for inappropriate ends. Equally, however, all over Europe, we in Britain as much as our fellow Europeans on the Continent, do indeed share common historical roots which are still discernible and which should be cherished to nurture new growth.

Notes and References

1 Johannes Rau, 'Ansprache', in *799 Kunst und Kultur der Karolingerzeit. Karl der Große und Papst Leo III in Paderborn. Ausstellungseröffnung am 23 Juli 1999 – Dokumentation* (Paderborn, 1999), p. 15.
2 W. Hentze (ed.), *De Karolo rege et Leone papa*, Studien und Quellen zur westfälischen Geschichte, 36 (Paderborn, 1999).
3 *Annales regnum francorum* s.a. 799, ed. F. Kurze, *MGH (Monumenta Germaniae Historica), Scriptores rerum germanicarum in usum scholarum* (Hannover, 1895), p. 106.
4 Trans. P. Godman, *Poetry of the Carolingian Renaissance* (London, 1985), p. 199.
5 *Ibid.*, p. 203.
6 Denys Hay, *Europe: The Emergence of an Idea* (Edinburgh, 1957).
7 Dicuil, *Liber de mensura orbis mensura*, ed. J.J. Tierney, *Scriptores Latini Hiberniae* (Dublin, 1967), p. 45.
8 See J.B. Harley and David Woodward, *The History of Cartography. Vol. I: Cartography in Prehistoric, Ancient and Medieval Europe and the Mediterranean* (Chicago, 1987), pp. 283–304.
9 Rosamond McKitterick, *The Frankish Kingdoms under the Carolingians, 751–987* (London, 1983), pp. 16–40; Ian Wood, *The Merovingian Kingdoms, 450–751* (London, 1994), pp. 255–92; and Paul Fouracre, *The Age of Charles Martel* (Harlow, 2000).
10 See Janet L. Nelson, *Politics and Ritual in Early Medieval Europe* (London, 1986), and Richard A. Jackson (ed.), *Ordines coronationis franciae. Texts and Ordines for the Coronation of Frankish and French Kings and Queens in the Middle Ages*, vol. 1 (Philadelphia, 1995).
11 McKitterick, *Frankish Kingdoms*, pp. 41–76; and see also P. Fouracre, 'Frankish Gaul to 814' in R. McKitterick (ed.), *The New Cambridge Medieval History, Vol. II: c. 700–c. 900* (Cambridge, 1995), pp. 85–109.
12 Günther Binding, *Deutsche Königspfalzen von Karl dem Grossen bis Friedrich II (765–1240)* (Darmstadt, 1996), and M. de Jong, F. Theuws and C. van Rhijn (eds), *Topographies of Power in the Early Middle Ages* (Leiden, 2001). For Frankish territorial divisions, see the maps in *The*

Times Atlas of European History, 2nd edn (London, 1998), for the year 565, pp. 54–5.

13 E. Ewig, 'Residence et capitale pendant le haut moyen âge', *Revue Historique*, 130 (1963), pp. 25–72, reprinted in E. Ewig, ed. H. Atsma, *Spätantikes und fränkisches Gallien. Gesammelte Schriften*, vol. 1 (Munich, 1976), pp. 362–408.

14 Georges Tessier, *La diplomatie royale française* (Paris, 1962).

15 Rosamond McKitterick, *The Carolingians and the Written Word* (Cambridge, 1989).

16 J.M. Wallace-Hadrill, *The Frankish Church* (Oxford, 1983).

17 Roger Wright, *Late Latin and Early Romance in Spain and Carolingian France* (Liverpool, 1982), Roger Wright (ed.), *Latin and the Romance Languages in the Early Middle Ages* (London, 1991), and Michel Banniard, 'Language and Communication in Carolingian Europe', in McKitterick (ed.), *The New Cambridge Medieval History*, vol. II, pp. 695–708.

18 On German see Cyril Edwards, 'German vernacular literature: A Survey', in Rosamond McKitterick (ed.), *Carolingian Culture: Emulation and Innovation* (Cambridge, 1994), pp. 141–70.

19 See all the essays in McKitterick, *Carolingian Culture*, as well as those by Contreni, Ganz and Nees in McKitterick (ed.), *New Cambridge Medieval History*, vol. II. In the following paragraphs I have drawn on my chapter 'Die karolingische Renovatio. Eine Einführung', in *799: Kunst und Kultur der Karolingerzeit*, ed. Christoph Stiegemann and Matthias Wemhoff (Paderborn, 1999), vol. 2, pp. 668–85. An extended version of that essay in English is to be published in J. Story (ed.), *Charlemagne* (Manchester, 2002).

20 Ed. A. Boretius, *MGH Capitularia*, vol. I (Hannover, 1886), no. 22, p. 60; English trans. David King, *Charlemagne. Translated Sources* (Kendal, 1987), p. 217.

21 *Ibid.*, no. 29, p. 79; English trans. King, *Translated Sources*, pp. 232–3.

22 See Richard Gameson (ed.), *The Early Medieval Bible: Its Production, Decoration and Use* (Cambridge, 1994).

23 Bernhard Bischoff, *Manuscripts and Libraries in the Age of Charlemagne* (Cambridge, 1994).

24 McKitterick, *Carolingians and the Written Word*, pp. 164–210.

25 Einhard, *Vita Karoli*, vol. 2, chs 25 and 26, ed. O. Holder-Egger, *MGH Scriptores rerum germanicarum in usum scholarum* (Hannover, 1911); English trans. P. Dutton, *Charlemagne's Courtier* (Peterborough, Ontario, 1998), pp. 32–3.

26 See Rosamond McKitterick, *History and its Audiences* (Cambridge, 2000), and the references there cited.

27 For an example of such opinion, characteristic of those schooled in the

perspectives of the twelfth century who may not have kept abreast of the scholarship of the past three decades or so, see the extraordinary recent comment by Martin Lhotzky that 'scarcely any of [Charlemagne's] reforms survived him, and many of his supposed deeds seem to have sprung from the vivid imagination of his adviser and biographer, Einhard', *Frankfurter Allgemeine Zeitung* (Culture and Society), 8 August 2001, 182, p. 7.

28 For Suger see Erwin Panofsky, *Abbot Suger on the Abbey Church of St-Denis and its Art Treasures*, 2nd edn (Princeton, 1979), and see also Ralph Glaber, *Historiarum libri quinque*, vol. III ch. 13, in *Rodulfus Glaber Opera*, ed. John France, Neithard Bulst and Paul Reynolds, Oxford Medieval Texts (Oxford, 1989), pp. 114–17.

29 See the chapters assessing the continuation into the eleventh century in Rosamond McKitterick (ed.), *The Short Oxford History of Europe: The Early Middle Ages* (Oxford, 2001).

30 Documented in detail in Philip Grierson and Mark Blackburn, *Medieval European Coinage, Vol. I: The Early Middle Ages (5th–10th Centuries)* (Cambridge, 1986).

31 On the coinage of Louis the Pious see S.C. Coupland, 'Money and Coinage under Louis the Pious', *Francia*, 17/1 (1990), pp. 23–54.

32 Sigebert of Gembloux, *Liber de scriptoribus ecclesiasticis*, ed. R. Witte, *Lateinische Sprache und Literatur des Mittelalters*, 1 (1974), and Honorius Augustodunensis, *De luminaribus ecclesiae*, *Patrologia Latina*, 172, ed. J.P. Migne (Paris, 1854), cols 197–234.

33 Robert Folz, *Études sur le culte liturgique de Charlemagne dans les églises de l'empire* (Paris, 1951).

34 See R. Folz, *Le souvenir et la légende de Charlemagne dans l'empire germanique médiéval* (Paris, 1950), *Gabáltais searluis móir* (The conquests of Charlemagne), ed. Douglas Hyde, Irish Texts Society (London, 1917), and K.-E. Geith, *Carolus Magnus. Studien zur Darstellung Karls des Großen in der deutschen Literatur des 12. und 13. Jahrhunderts* (Munich, 1977).

35 Robert Peril, *La genealogie et descente de la tres illustre maison Dautriche* (Antwerp, 1535). See Jürgen Voss, *Das Mittelalter im historischen Denken Frankreichs. Untersuchung zur Geschichte des Mittelalterbegriffes und der Mittelalterbewertung von der zweiten Hälfte des 16. bis zur Mitte des 19. Jahrhunderts* (Munich, 1972), and Rosamond McKitterick, 'The Study of Frankish History in France and Germany in the Sixteenth and Seventeenth Centuries', *Francia*, 8 (1980), pp. 556–72.

36 A useful introduction is Robert Folz, *The Concept of Empire in Western Europe from the Fifth to the Fourteenth Century* (London, 1969, from 1953 French edition).

37 *Vita Karoli*, II, ch. 31, English trans, Dutton, *Charlemagne's Courtier*, p. 36.

38 Thietmar von Merseburg, *Chronicon*, IV, ch. 47, ed. Robert Holtzmann, *MGH Scriptores rerum germanicarum, new series*, 9 (Berlin, 1935), p. 184, and English trans. David Warner, *Ottonian Germany: The Chronicon of Thietmar of Merseburg* (Manchester, 2001), p. 185.

39 *799: Kunst und Kultur der Karolingerzeit*, 2, pp. 758–63.

40 See *Krönungen. Könige in Aachen – Geschichte und Mythos. Katalog der Austellung*, ed. Mario Kramp (Mainz, 2000), and François Macé de Lépinay, *Peintures et sculptures du Panthéon* (Paris, 1997), pp. 36–7.

41 Still a useful account is David Knowles, *Great Historical Enterprises* (London, 1963).

42 See Ian Wood, 'Report: The European Science Foundation's Programme on the Transformation of the Roman World and Emergence of Early Medieval Europe', *Early Medieval Europe*, 6 (1997), pp. 217–28, and the series of volumes now being published by Brill in Leiden. One of the five exhibitions organized in conjunction with the project was *The Transformation of the Roman World* at the British Museum and (former) British Library: see the exhibition catalogue, ed. L. Webster and M. Brown (London, 1997).

43 See the maps and supporting texts in *The Times Atlas of European History*, 2nd edn (London, 1997), pp. 60–2, 144–7, 188–91, and R. Overy (ed.), *The Times Atlas of World History* 5th edn (London, 1999).

44 For apposite commentary, see Patrick J. Geary, *The Myth of Nations: The Medieval Origins of Europe* (Princeton, 2002).

JONATHAN STEINBERG

What is Europe?

In the autumn of 1994 I taught at several universities in Lithuania. In one of my lectures, I asked my audience how they defined Europe. They answered, 'Everything west of the border with Belarus.' Europe for them meant the West with a capital W, the Latin script, their independence from the Soviet Union and their membership in some wider, non-Slavic community like the European Union. Now I teach at the University of Pennsylvania. Many of my students were born in Korea, Taiwan, Vietnam or the Indian subcontinent; their first languages are not European and they know little or nothing of the elements of European history or culture. These two very different audiences – the Eastern European and the Asian-American – have made me think again about what Europe is and why it matters. Europe is not simply a geographical term like 'Australia' or 'Antarctica', nor is it some general phenomenon like 'globalization' or 'fundamentalism'. 'Europe' stands for both the geographical area and the culture or civilization which has evolved in that space and which has, for good or ill, spread its ways via conversion, colonialism and capitalism to much, if not all, of the world. 'Europe' embodies principles or values which distinguish it from Asia, the Americas, Africa and Australasia. Brazil is not a European country though its culture has strong roots in the Iberian peninsula. When West Indians play cricket on Sunday in Philadelphia's Fairmount Park, they do not become Europeans at the wicket. But the influence of Europe in both cases is undeniable.

The pervasiveness of European identity, indeed, the power of that identity to leave institutional traces on every place it touches, the energy that drove Spanish monks to bring the cross to the heathen across the jungles and deserts of the New World or that drove German Anabaptists to carve homesteads in the North American woods or that led merchant adventurers to ship spices and slaves across vast oceans, belong to the definition too. Europe's wars, its technologies of destruction, its revolutions and secular ideologies, its variety and turbulence, its high culture and low life, all that reverberates in the word and in the question 'What is Europe?'

Thinking on the scale required to answer a really big question like 'What is Europe?' requires a few introductory words about method. Historical statements, whether very general or specific, are not susceptible to proof criteria of the kind found in the natural sciences. The historian cannot re-run the French Revolution with the variables altered. There is only one past and it no longer exists. It has left its memories, artifacts and testimonies in varying degrees of density. Understanding the past involves different techniques from those used in laboratory sciences and different arguments from those advanced in mathematics, theoretical physics or the purer forms of philosophy. As Dr Johnson shrewdly observed, 'Great abilities are not requisite for an historian: for in historical composition all the greatest powers of the human mind are quiescent.'[1]

By comparison with the powers of thought required to solve Fermat's last theorem or write *The General Theory of Employment, Interest and Money*, historians hardly think at all. We collect data, file and organize it, put it into intelligible prose and, with luck, drop it onto a market already groaning under the weight of too many books. But some process of thought does occur and, I believe, one peculiar to our craft.

It has been my experience that historians only know what they think when they have completed writing their texts and by then it is too late to alter. My brief experience as expert witness in a war crimes trial reinforced that view. The prosecution only knew what missing evidence would have been necessary to convict the accused when it was too late to find it. Historians, like lawyers, deal with an infinite number of 'facts' (however defined) that are in principle knowable. Deciding which are relevant may require, as Johnson put it, 'some penetration, accuracy and colouring' plus a small admixture of imagination, 'about as much as is used in the lower forms of poetry',[2] but the choice of relevant fact is at least partly a random outcome of what the historians have unearthed or simply what has survived.

When historians turn from their microscopic examinations of specific events or phenomena to ask large questions like 'What is Europe?' their method does not change nor do they get any smarter. The basic proposition of all historical enquiry continues to obtain: *a historical statement is one which in principle is or should be refutable*. If in what follows I assert that Europe has certain properties, the reader should be able to say 'Nonsense, because . . .' If he/she can, we are doing history, however macroscopic the scale; if not, I have wandered beyond the borders of an empirical enquiry and have begun to do something other than history. I will not, therefore, talk of a European 'spirit' nor cite inherent or innate tendencies. When I use the word 'culture', I mean those works, ideas, habits, forms of speech, written languages and spoken dialects, religious beliefs and practices and so on, which are observable in various communities at various times in what has become known as the European subcontinent.

There is, nevertheless, one aspect of our subject which violates the principle of refutability: *knowledge specific to us by our membership in a species of communicating animals*. By specifically human knowledge I mean the knowledge that arises between communicating persons: you meet somebody and you sense that he dislikes you or you suddenly inexplicably dislike him; the feeling of alarm that a letter may evoke which you cannot entirely explain; the sudden insight into a colleague's character; the fleeting look of distrust on the face of somebody at a meeting. None of these signals are refutable but all register on our invisible antennae as part of human communication. We depend on the knowledge that such communication affords whether we know it consciously or not. Communication from past human beings – the stuff of historical research – works that way too. We come to 'know' Philip II or Bismarck by studying their writing. We are moved, repelled, attracted, etc., by that knowledge. The two propositions – refutability and human knowledge – fit uneasily with each other but they make up in my opinion the core of historical method. It is philosophically messy to have to work with both, but not messier than the life itself which the historian observes.

The geographer E.L. Jones describes European development as a 'miracle'.[3] He argues that Europe had a variety of geopolitical characteristics that distinguished it as an environment. It lacked great areas subject to flooding or monsoon and hence avoided the endemic infection of the rice paddies and water-based agricultures. The cold, rainy climate reduced the multiplication of harmful microbes and the east–west axes of the mountain ranges reduced sharply the number of plants and animal species which survived the last ice age. Hence the number of poisonous insects, snakes and plants was lower in Europe than elsewhere. The European coast has an unusually high number of bays, fjords, inlets and seas which means that the coast–inland ratio is high and fish-culture and fish protein have been unusually plentiful and easily reached. He then suggests that good diet, better health and environment led to very different family size, age of marriage and population densities from that seen elsewhere.[4] Europeans were less numerous than Asians, healthier and more independent. The individual embodied a higher economic cost–benefit quota and could extract correspondingly better terms from landlords and princes. Hence, Jones argues, European agriculture became relatively more capital-intensive and labour-saving from an early date by comparison with other civilizations.

Michael Mann adds a technological dimension to geography. The water wheel, the heavy plough, horse-shoes and leather harnesses permitted Europeans to cultivate much heavier, mineral-rich soils than elsewhere and to arrive well before 1000 AD at 'an entirely novel system of agriculture'. He shows that at the time of the Domesday Book the Normans counted 6000 water mills, roughly one for every ten to thirty people, which in turn allowed a very decentralized economy to emerge.[5] Europe developed as a network of semi-autonomous, self-regulating communities, a kind of bee-hive structure, in which collective decisions could be made on local level. Communal cultivation and decision-making distinguished Alpine regions from an early date, as did a high degree of specialization in dairy and meat production.[6]

The question where this relatively individualistic, productive and varied agriculture ended cannot be easily answered. In eastern Poland and beyond the Carpathians, the land flattens out and turns into the endlessness of Russian steppe culture. Whether geography alone explains the spread of the serf economy and its durability is a question well beyond my competence but the theorists of the centre–periphery argument would point to the revival of serfdom in early modern times as an example of market forces in the West and corresponding responses in the East: the spread of the great estate and the increase in cereal production which it allowed.

The geopolitical and economic elements interacted with the very peculiar legacy of the Roman Empire. Here we must survey the entire course of European history from the fall of the Roman Empire to the adoption of the Euro. In these nearly sixteen centuries all attempts to impose uniformity from above have failed. From Charlemagne to Hitler the dream of 'ein Reich, ein Volk, ein Führer' has turned into a nightmare. Europeans resisted it and in the end succeeded. The great Chinese empire managed to impose uniformity – give or take the odd period of war lords – for thousands of years. The khans, moghuls and sultans imposed uniform rules within the limits of their technology. Emperors, kings and dictators in Europe could not. The roots of this failure lie in the peculiar Roman, Christian and feudal inheritance which made Europe unlike any other part of the world.

When the Roman Empire disintegrated, it left an unusual legacy, the image of a world empire which was at the same time a city, a polis, an entity composed of citizens who had laws, votes, plebiscites, senates, consuls and all the rest of Roman republican paraphernalia. No other world empire had those features. Roman law embodied them and passed it to us today through the conduit of Latin Christianity and humanist scholarship. There is scarcely a word in our political vocabulary, starting with the words 'political' and 'vocabulary' themselves, that cannot be traced back to the Roman republic or its predecessor, the Greek city-state.

This civic practice of free Romans rested on slavery. Citizens, those to whom Socrates put hard questions and Cicero made great speeches, belonged to a privileged minority who depended on institutional inequalities to enjoy the *otium* or leisure which the *res publica* required. In its later years the Roman inheritance got mixed up with the very different values of the Judaeo-Christian prophecies. The Old Testament prophets condemned 'those that oppress the hireling in his wages'. The prophet Malachi asked 'Have we not all one father? Hath not one God created us?' (Malachi 3:5 and 2:10) This message of the equality of all men became one of the central precepts of the Good

News of Jesus Christ that the last shall be first, that the poor are particularly blessed and that in a famous image 'it is easier for a camel to go through the eye of a needle, than for a rich man to enter the Kingdom of God'. The Roman Catholic church which survived and preserved the Roman civic inheritance transmitted both Latin civic culture and its imperial aspirations but also the revolutionary egalitarianism of Jewish and Christian prophesy to Europe. 'When Adam delved and Eve span, who was then the gentleman?' asked the peasants who rebelled in England in 1381. Judaeo-Christian egalitarianism planted a ticking bomb at the base of every European authority, whether religious or secular. St Francis, Savonarola, Martin Luther, the Anabaptists, the *Enragés* of 1792, the utopians of the nineteenth century, the anarchists, communists, hippies and demonstrators outside the IMF conferences of our own time, continue in varying ways to try to fulfil that ancient prophesy, where indeed the last shall be first.

The final peculiarity of European history is feudalism, that curious disintegration of central authority which occurred only in Europe, early modern Japan and nowhere else. The two feudal systems arose when the emperor's authority fell into bits. Great lords took chunks of imperial power and, in order to sustain their new authority, had to make deals with lesser lords and they in turn with even lesser lords down to the base of society. In the Latin West but not in the Greek or Russian Orthodox East, there emerged a thicket of rights, privileges, exemptions, contractual agreements out of which the Swiss cantons and other European polities emerged. The struggle to regain central control over the disintegrated imperial possessions, the battles between princes and their *Stände* or estates, between cities and their guilds, between churches and their tenants, between peasant communities and their lords, became the structural reality of Europe from the eleventh century to last week. These struggles used the language of Roman law and civic individualism but also of Christian justice and egalitarianism. In this millennial struggle, by accident, good fortune, geography and the interests of the surrounding princes, bits and pieces like Liechtenstein, the Swiss Confederation, the Grand Duchy of Luxemburg survived into the modern era as the last, decentralized, self-governing territories of old Europe.

A critical stage in the struggle between authority from above and resistance from below was the combined impact of the printing press and the Protestant Reformation. The Word had been made print. The impact of that democratization of doctrine is with us still in the dozens of subdivisions in which Protestant believers have divided and the extremely fine readings of the Bible that give rise to those divisions. Once Everyman became his own priest, the struggle to impose uniformity from above was doomed from the start but it took a century and a half of war, plague and pestilence before that obvious fact could be accepted. Europe had now become even more fragmented and the fragments throbbed with their own individual religious identities.

The explosion of European colonial expansion, which in part financed those wars, created huge opportunities for Europeans to get rich, spread their religions, escape persecution, convert or exterminate the previous inhabitants and disseminate their diseases. New Spains, New Portugals, New Frances, New Amsterdams and New Yorks began to grow on remote coastlines and the Europeans dialects became world languages. The sense that Europeans had some common identity began to emerge in contact with existing great civilizations and brought alternative ways of thought and practice back to the so-called 'old countries'. Whether the influences came from new products such as tobacco or new ideas, as in the Jesuit experiments in Paraguay, or with Chinese rites, they enriched and subtly transformed the European self-definition. At the same time the new technologies of seafaring, navigation, telescopes and microscopes gave Europe in the seventeenth century the bases on which a world no longer magical but much larger than previously imagined could be dissected, analysed and tamed. Newton and Pascal, Descartes and Leibniz set the stage for a new and uniquely European secular philosophy. Hume, Adam Smith, Rousseau and Kant worked through the implications of a world no longer unified by Christian authority.

Secular uniformity proved equally illusive. How far enlightened rationalism penetrated cannot be easily determined but in the French Revolution it became the secular religion of the greatest European state. French revolutionaries promised careers open to talent, uniformity of weights and measures, equality before the law, abolition of guilds and ghettos and declared war on monarchy and aristocracy. French troops flattened the existing borders of the surviving feudal principalities, duchies and princely bishoprics, and French agents swept away what they regarded as the rubbish of history. Once again European identity from below rose to resist the imposition of uniformity. These 'enemies of progress' fought the French from the tip of the Italian peninsula to the Vendée.

Liberalism and nationalism had no more success than the French in imposing a uniform code of belief on Europe. Nation-states, though regarded in the nineteenth century as the final stage of human development, turned out to be unsatisfactory for some of their new subjects. The speakers of other languages and dialects, the practitioners of minority religions, found the nation-state's claim to uniformity intolerable. The *Kulturkampf*, which pitted the new nation-state in Germany, Italy or France against the old Roman Catholic Church, ended in defeat or truce. The state could not exterminate 'superstition' and the Church could not defeat 'godless liberalism'. Neither could prevent the rise of industralization and the spread of yet another uniform and unifying ideology: Marxist socialism. The peculiar historical irony which made the ideology of progress the governing doctrine of the least progressive state in Europe, tsarist Russia, is well known. The terrible industrialized mass murder of the First World War is also known, though in its full impact still not entirely charted. Yet again grandiose unifying ideologies emerged, partly in reaction to the Bolshevik version of Marxism and partly from deep currents in many European states which hated and feared the 'modern' world of industrial production and uniform consumption. Fascism, National Socialism and Bolshevism continued the French Revolutionary crusade to create by political means and police repression a new human being in a new society. Again the attempt to impose these projects on the European subcontinent failed amid further slaughter, desolation and hopelessness. The end of the Eastern Bloc in 1989/1991 marked the end of that era of political experimentation and the hope of human perfectability. Out of the rubble of the Marxist–Leninist establishments, the old identities appeared again.

The essence of Europe and the answer to our question can begin to be seen in this constant turbulence. Europe bubbles with energy from below and that bubbling confronts rigidities from above. Europe resembles an enormous structure of units of different size and properties which never reaches equilibrium. The little entities of Europe are part of its vitality and there is a sense in which 'What is Europe?' can be best answered by their example. The one I have chosen is the Italian-speaking Canton of Ticino. If we can understand why this tiny speck of Italian culture zealously guards its independence, we can see a feature of Europe which accounts for much of its peculiar restlessness. Tiny, apparently irrelevant nuclei of local identity simply resist the attempt to co-ordinate and eliminate them from above. What gives them the energy and tenacity to remain independent? This is, in effect, part of the answer to the question 'What is Europe?'

Ticino calls itself officially the Republic and Canton of Ticino and, like every modern state, has a proper constitution. The preamble to the Ticino Constitution of 1997, states:

> The Ticinese people [il popolo ticinese] in order to guarantee peaceful life together with respect for the dignity of man, fundamental liberties and social justice; convinced that these ideals realize themselves in a democratic community of citizens which seek the common good; faithful to its historic task to interpret Italian culture within the Helvetic Confederation; conscious that its responsibility towards future generations requires sustainable human activity with respect to nature and a use of human knowledge which respects man and the universe; ordains for itself the following Constitution:

> Article 1
> 1. The Canton Ticino is a democratic republic of Italian culture and language.
> 2. The Canton is a member of the Swiss Confederation and its sovereignty [sovranità] is limited only by the Federal Constitution.

What extraordinary claims: *sovranità, il popolo ticinese*. Is there such a thing? Does the *popolo ticinese* claim its rights alongside the American people or the people of China? How many *Ticinesi* are there? According to official figures, there are 306,179 inhabitants of this republic of whom 73.8 per cent or 225,960 are citizens. The Republic has a total area of 2,812 square kilometers, contains 245 municipalities with an average population of 1,245 inhabitants per commune and its biggest city is Lugano with a population of 25,771.[7] In other words, the total population of the sovereign Republic and canton of Ticino is less than that of the city of Zurich. This mini-state gives itself a constitution, a flag, a legal code, a parliament, an executive and a judiciary. It claims to be sovereign when it occupies no more than a speck on the map.

This tiny state faces the prospect of being swallowed by the surrounding European union of states and, as the referendum on 4 March 2001 showed, it does not like it. Only 15.9 per cent of those who voted in Ticino said 'yes' to immediate negotiations to join the European Union, well below the already low national average of 23.3 per cent.[8] From the outside, this behaviour looks distinctly odd. In the age of globalization, Ticino demands its independence. It seems to say 'no' to what more than 300 million fellow-Europeans regard as the future: an integrated federal European Union with its currency, its mobile defence forces and, if the foreign minister of the Federal Republic of Germany has his way, its own constitution.

Why should Ticino continue to exist? After all, the disappearance of states has precedents in European history. The Serene Republic of Venice disappeared on 12 May 1797, when Bonaparte abolished it, and Venice was larger, richer and more important than Ticino. The German Democratic Republic with all its institutions and its immense secret police network disappeared in eleven months in 1989–90 like a mirage and left literally nothing behind except seventeen million confused citizens and 200 kilometres of Stasi files on them. What would the Republic and Canton of Ticino leave for posterity? Who would even notice that it had gone?

Why should it survive? First and most important, the people concerned want it that way, and they have done so for many years. In 1796, the Bernese aristocrat Karl-Viktor von Bonstetten made his annual inspection trip to Lugano, then a subject territory under the control of the thirteen cantons of the Old Confederation. He did not like what he saw. The entire region was badly governed 'organized ideally for evil, where the good is impossible'. The head of government was the *Landvogt* or bailiff, who, as von Bonstetten noted,

was judge of life and death. Uncountable are the abuses of such a regime. In no corner of Europe, no matter how dismal, has torture raged so wildly as in Italian Switzerland. The *Landvogt*, who had no salary, had to live off fines (that is, pecuniary punishments) and with these he compensated for . . . the corruptions with which his office had been purchased.[9]

Under such a dreadful regime, it was hardly surprising that some local enthusiasts took up the cause of progress and the French Revolution, declared themselves patriots and friends of the people, and demanded that the Italian-speaking valleys of the Swiss Confederation rebel and join the new French Cisalpine Republic. On 15 February 1798 the patriots attempted a *coup d'état* and proclaimed the union of Ticino to the French puppet state. To their dismay, the crowd that gathered in the Piazza Grande in Lugano shouted them down, demanded that the representatives of Unterwalden whom the patriots had seized be released and that the patriots leave town, which they did in some confusion. That evening two lawyers from Ponte Tresa, Annibale Pellegrini and Angelo Stoppani, led a group of armed men to the representatives from Unterwalden, who were, after all, their oppressors, and demanded not French but Swiss liberty: 'We demand our sacred rights; we desire Swiss liberty; finally after centuries of subjection, we are mature enough to govern ourselves.'[10] When the representatives of Unterwalden promised to carry that message back to the Confederation, celebrations began. The crowd planted a Tree of Liberty, adorned it with a William Tell cap, and shouted that they were '*Svizzeri e Liberi*'.

Swiss liberty was not French liberty. The Swiss rejected then as they do now the uniform, centralized, rational and faceless version of liberty which the Jacobin clubs in Paris preached and the French state practised. Its successor, the French-dominated European Union, continues to struggle for that one indivisible, uniform bureaucratic paradise where all children study the same subject at the same hour in every school, where all bananas curve at the same angle and uniform rules govern the amount of vegetable oil found in chocolate from the Arctic Circle to the Straits of Gibraltar. This vision of perfect uniformity has shaped the so-called *acquis communautaire*, that bundle of Euro-regulations to be applied in every member state and to be imposed in their entirety on every potential member. That is the price expected of Switzerland for the privilege of membership of the

European Union. Eighty-five per cent of the Ticinesi who voted in March 2001 said no to French liberty as their forefathers had done two centuries before.

Switzerland still has enclaves and exclaves, bits of territory which belong to one canton but remain obstinately lodged in the territory of another. This oddity, the last remnant of the old Holy Roman Empire from which Switzerland emerged, preserves the sovereignty and wishes of often very tiny communities. In this respect it embodies the '*Europe des Patries*' or the '*Europe des Régions*' or, in my terms, that essential tension between top-down and bottom-up which distinguishes European history and identity.

Swiss liberty meant to the Ticinesi of 1798 the preservation of that ancient set of local rights, feudal exemptions and privileges which history had bequeathed to them. They sometimes spoke the language of universal rights but they understood them in a very particular way. However modern, environmentally and politically correct the Ticino Constitution of 1997 may sound, it rests on a much older, much less obvious and much less common sense of liberty than that on which most other European states base their legitimacy. We can call it 'particular liberty' as opposed to the 'universal liberty' which the French Revolution or the UN Declaration on Human Rights proclaimed as valid for everybody, everywhere and at all times.

The Swiss Confederation and the Republic and Canton of Ticino embody their variant of 'particular liberty', although being Swiss they neither think about it much nor care. That's just the way things are because they have always been that way. They should think about it because particular liberty provides a way to answer the question 'What is Europe?' This answer is not some Burkean conservatism which attacks the age of reason and the tradition of European Enlightenment in favour of antiquated views and reactionary practice. Nor is it the populist xenophobic particularism of a Christoph Blocher or a Jörg Haider. Real civic particular liberty reminds our bureaucratic masters that, as Thomas Jefferson aptly put it, 'the people are happier of themselves than in the care of wolves'. It reminds the civil servants and politicians that mistakes made from below have a legitimacy which mistakes made from above never have. If they want us to do something, then let us discuss it in our local communities and then vote on it: in other words, the Swiss tradition of direct democracy.

The famous 'winds of change' that Harold Macmillan felt when Africa began to stir are beginning to blow from an unexpected direction, one quite helpful to the Republic and Canton of Ticino. Globalization has had the paradoxical effect of stirring up particularisms of all kinds. Small nationalities emerge and even smaller ones follow them. The Russian doll has turned out, especially in the former Soviet Union, to be a perfect image of that process. Inside every nationality, a smaller one is trying to get out. The growth of European integration has weakened the nation-state. Scotland, Wales, Catalonia, the Basque Country, Friesland, the Faroes, Lombardy, the Veneto, Brittany and so on are beginning to ask why they should not be the sovereign unit, and the answer has yet to be formulated. Subsidiarity, 'Europe of the regions' and the cacophony of reactions to such ideas indicate that the existing structures are creaking.

That tension is not new. The secret of Europe has always been, as I have tried to show, the tension between universal and particular, between the empire and the estates, between the princes and their towns, between universalist religious claims and sectarian practice, between universal values and particular rights. That constant irritating, relentless but ultimately creative struggle has made Europe the vital, vigorous, inexhaustibly interesting place that it is. That is why the Republic and Canton of Ticino and that group whom the constitution calls '*il popolo ticinese*' continues to exist. Within the boundaries of Canton Ticino, even smaller units, its own regions, the Mendrisiotto, the Locarnese, the Luganese and so on, continue to battle for resources and to maintain even smaller identities. The tension between universal and particular, between centre and periphery, between federal and state power, may not always be comfortable to live with but it is the very core of European identity. That is what Europe is.

Notes and References

1 James Boswell, *Life of Johnson*, ed. R.W. Chapman (Oxford: Oxford University Press, 1970), Wednesday 6 July, 1763, p. 301.
2 *Ibid.*, p. 301.

3 E.L. Jones, *The European Miracle: Environments, Economies and Geopolitics in the History of Europe and Asia*, 2nd edn (Cambridge, 1987).

4 *Ibid.*, table 1.1, p. 17, and table 12.1, p. 232.

5 Michael Mann, 'European Development. Approaching a Historical Explanation', in J. Baechler, J.A. Holl and M. Mann (ed.), *Europe and the Rise of Capitalism* (Oxford: Blackwell, 1988), pp. 6–19.

6 J. Steinberg, *Why Switzerland?* (Cambridge: Cambridge University Press, 2nd edn, 1996), p. 17.

7 Cantone Ticino – SPEL-Copernico – 1.3 Canton Ticino in Figures http://www.ti.ch/DFE/DE/SPEL.

8 *Neue Zürcher Zeitung* 'NZZ–On Line', 6 March, 2001http://www.nzz.ch/.

9 Karl Viktor von Bonstetten, *Lettere sopra i baliaggi italiani*, trans. Renato Martinoni (Locarno: Armando Dado, 1984), pp. 140–41.

10 Steinberg, *Why Switzerland?*, pp. 11—12.

TONY WRIGLEY

Production and Reproduction:
The Significance of Population History

In 1970 Peter Mathias delivered his inaugural lecture as Chichele
Professor of Economic History at Oxford. He entitled it 'Living with
the Neighbours: The Role of Economic History'. The issues which he
then went on to discuss reflected his particular concerns at the time,
but his title would be appropriate for the discussion of the role of
almost any branch of historical study. History is an outward-looking
subject, continually and necessarily in contact with its neighbours.
Any historian who is concerned with the wellsprings of motivation,
for example, must share borderlands with psychology; or, if an
historian wishes to achieve a better understanding of institutional
structures, he or she will be apt to find interests in common with some
aspects of sociology, anthropology and political science; and so on. A
degree of common interest and cross-fertilization is certain and often
of great benefit.

Offering some reflections on population history affords a further
opportunity to pursue this theme. Population history is part of what
might be termed the borderland between the social and the biological.
As with other animals, it has always been a condition of continued
existence for men that each generation should find means to ensure
that it is replaced by a new generation. In exploring this issue, much
which is of fundamental importance to the study of societies in the
past comes into focus. The nature of the demographic regimes of
societies in the past heavily conditioned other aspects of their life by
imposing certain characteristic constraints upon individuals, families,

the local community whether in town or country, and the larger political entities in which societies were organized. It is a particular merit of discussing this theme that it brings vividly to light both the scale and the nature of the great gulf which divides the pre-industrial world from the world which has developed in the more recent past. Over the past two centuries there has been fundamental change. Understanding this better should serve to clarify the nature of the world which is emerging on the brink of a new millennium.

The fundamental point can be put very simply. As a condition of continued survival, man must both produce and reproduce. In this humankind is on a par with all other animal species. Individual life will not continue unless basic needs, above all basic nutritional needs, are met, nor will it continue unless the next generation is as large as or larger than its predecessor on average. If successive generations are consistently smaller than their predecessors, self-evidently the community or species in question will disappear (though migration can complicate this assertion in particular localities). By reproduction, I mean the process by which one generation replaces another, rather than having in mind the more restricted sense in which it is sometimes used which relates exclusively to fertility. Mortality is just as important as fertility in determining the reproductive success of the group. By production I mean the process by which the material wants of a community are met. The four most basic of these needs have long been defined as food, clothing, shelter, and fuel, and these four dominated the production scene in every society until recently. Far enough back in human history the two imperatives to produce and to reproduce were just as stark for men as for any other animal species and very similar in character. It is not difficult to recognize the truth of this assertion in relation to hunter/fisher/gatherer communities but it remained true of the communities which developed in the wake of the neolithic food revolution and which practised settled agriculture. It is no accident that the only plea which relates to the material things of life in the Lord's Prayer should be that we should receive each day our daily bread: a blessing which can now be taken for granted, but this is a privilege confined to recent generations. In a sense the two imperatives remain powerful, but we shall see that the terms of the equation have changed radically in recent centuries.

Understanding what was once the case and what has changed is best approached, though not necessarily best understood, by reminding ourselves of the argument which occurred to Malthus when he was searching for a crushing rejoinder to those like Condorcet and Godwin, and his own father, who were inspired and attracted by the events of 1789 in France and who were convinced of the perfectibility of man and of human institutions. Malthus developed a line of argument which not only infuriated the radicals of his time because they found it so difficult to refute but may be the only major instance of a concept developed by a social scientist which played a significant part in the development of a natural science, for it was reading the *Essay on Population* which provided Darwin with the engine he needed to drive the process of natural selection.[1] Natural selection, which arises from an essentially Malthusian tension between production (food availability) and reproduction (the capacity of a population to increase in favourable circumstances), acted as the 'invisible hand' which could serve to explain both the development of differentiated species and their conjunction as a functioning ecological community in any particular period, much as the operation of the market, Adam Smith's 'invisible hand', could produce order and an efficient outcome from a welter of conflicting interests and imperfect knowledge.

Malthus's *Essay on Population* (1798) dealt with the interplay of production and reproduction. Malthus postulated that the ability of a society to increase its supply of food was at best to be represented as an arithmetic progression, 1, 2, 3, 4, 5, etc. Since food was necessary to sustain life this implied that the increase in population must be similarly limited, but the human reproductive process, like that of every other animal, was such that, unchecked, population would rise not arithmetically but geometrically, 1, 2, 4, 8, 16, etc. The demonstration that this was not an idle speculation lay immediately to hand in the experience of the American colonies in the seventeenth and eighteenth centuries where population had doubled in each successive generation, and had done so principally by natural increase, immigration having only a limited role in this regard.[2] In contrast, the English population had increased only modestly, though the two populations were essentially similar in their institutional structures, religious belief and social practices. In one case there was, for a time at least, an unlimited supply of new land to be taken up: in the other, a land already fully settled for a millennium. There was, Malthus

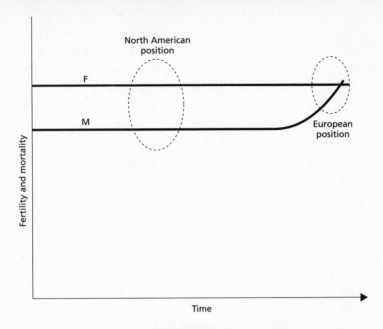

Figure 1: The relative positions of 'North American' and 'European' populations in a Malthusian world

argued, a necessary, inherent tension between the propensity of a population to grow and the ability of any given land surface to support additional population, and in consequence there must tend to be widespread poverty and a host of linked disabilities for the majority of mankind. The nature of the tension is particularly easy to grasp if set out graphically as in Figure 1.

In a highly simplified Malthusian setting, where the land is the source not only of food but of the great bulk of all the material products of use to man, fertility is assumed to be invariant and significantly higher than mortality as long as fertile land remains available to be taken up and material resources are therefore relatively abundant. Thus the English settlements in North America could grow rapidly since for many generations the growth in question caused no pressure upon the available resources. In contrast population growth in Europe was necessarily slow and uncertain because all good land had long been taken up and population could grow no faster than any increase in the productivity of the relatively fixed area of agricultural land. Where this was the case, mortality must at some point rise to the same level as fertility because population cannot outstrip accessible resources. As Malthus always recognized, it is, of course, arbitrary and often unrealistic to assume invariant fertility. And further, as Malthus also recognized, even in his initial formulation of the issue, the position is complicated by the fact that advances in technology imply that there is not a fixed ceiling to population growth, but one which may rise gradually over time. However, as long as the rate at which a population can rise in favourable circumstances exceeds the rate at which the economy can be expanded, the problem remains. Relative to available land, and hence to the ability to sustain population growth, therefore, the positions of England and of her North American colonies in the later eighteenth century would be as indicated on Figure 1. It came as a marked surprise to Malthus when the 1801 census revealed conclusively that population growth in England was rapid and accelerating. It was one of the reasons why he significantly changed his original stance on the issues of production and reproduction.

The *Essay on Population* was an immature exercise written with a particular polemical object in mind, a *pièce d'occasion*. In later life Malthus, who went to great trouble to improve his knowledge both of fact and theory, modified his views very substantially.[3] Even so, with the benefit of a knowledge of later events, his prognostications seem far wide of the mark. Yet he has much to say that is very relevant to an understanding of production and reproduction in traditional societies, though its relevance has tended to become obscured by the fact that he described a world which was on the point of transformation, a transformation which was to render both his initial, naive analysis and his later much more sophisticated modelling of reality largely inapplicable to events in the industrializing world of the nineteenth and twentieth centuries.

Consider first what constitute the strengths of the Malthusian analysis of traditional societies before turning to a discussion of the reasons why his ideas have largely ceased to be relevant. Malthus emphasized the degree of common ground between mankind and other animal species. For every animal species the scale of accessible food supplies sets a limit to the size of the population of that species which can be sustained in a given area. Herds of wildebeest cannot expand beyond the limits set by grazing capacity. The number of vultures is necessarily limited by the quantity of carrion which is locally available. Competition for food is inherent to such a situation. It is, at least as an acceptable approximation, a zero sum game. What you eat I cannot have and vice versa. As long as human societies were sustained by hunting, fishing and gathering, their situation was essentially similar to that of any other animal species, except that occasional technological advances broadened the range of accessible food from time to time. With a bow and arrow rather than a club there is an increase in the variety and size of game animals which can be attacked with hope of success. The advent of settled agriculture and domesticated farm animals initially lifted the population ceiling dramatically. Whereas previously edible vegetable supplies depended upon the natural frequency of the plants in question in the vegetation complex, now huge tracts of land were denuded of their natural vegetation to be replaced by a very limited number of plants useful to man. The replacement of wild by domesticated animals is in essence a similar story.

The same point can be expressed differently. Photosynthesis underlies all life. It is the basis of vegetable growth and thus, indirectly, of all life, since plant growth forms the base of the food chain sustaining animals, birds, insects, fish and so on. Human groups, through the neolithic food revolution, learned how to divert a much larger percentage of the products of photosynthesis for their exclusive use than they were able to secure in a hunter/fisher/gatherer setting. However, the neolithic food revolution did not significantly change the scale of photosynthesis worldwide. It only annexed a larger percentage for human use. In other words, the ceiling was greatly raised, but there remained a ceiling, and once population had expanded to a new and higher level it met again the same fundamental difficulty, the difficulty which Malthus had captured in his exposition of the contrast between arithmetic and geometric powers of growth.

So far we have an instructive truism to take on board, but not one which takes analysis very far. However, Malthus laid the foundations for an extension of his basic insight which has proved very productive. First, reference should be made to a complication of which he was well aware and which, as already noted, modifies the simplicity of the general principle. The relationship between carrying capacity and numbers in animal species is, in a sense, absolute. Each successive generation of animals faces identical tensions in the competition for food to those experienced by its predecessor. But in human societies changes in technology modify this simple picture. This was true of pre-agricultural societies, as we noted in the case of the bow and arrow, but was more evidently true of agricultural societies. Examples abound. The development of increasingly sophisticated methods of irrigation can transform the productivity of arid land. The introduction of an iron-shod plough share can greatly change the ease of cultivating the soil, as can the use of a horse harness which does not slowly strangle the animal when it leans into its work. The list could be extended virtually indefinitely. The significance of technological change is even clearer in relation to industrial production than in reference to agriculture. Nevertheless agricultural societies did not manage to escape the fundamental problem by such means, only to alleviate difficulties temporarily.

But there is another side to this issue, which Malthus helped to clarify, and which was, arguably, of even greater importance. The fact that a ceiling exists does not mean that different populations will approach that ceiling equally closely. A population which presses hard against the ceiling will, *ceteris paribus*, be one in which a large proportion of the population lives on the margin of existence, vulnerable to the random impact of harvest fluctuations and other unpredictable events. A population which develops characteristics which are likely to arrest growth well short of the notional ceiling may be substantially more cushioned against such events. By definition, in all populations the bare necessities of life must be available to the bulk of the population for most of the time, but in a population which limits population growth effectively, what the classical economists referred to as the comforts of life may be accessible to many people, and even the luxuries of life to more than a few. In the circumstances of agricultural societies, whether the people were successful in avoiding the miseries which attended exuberant population growth depended in large part on their social conventions, an issue which Malthus examined even in the first edition of the *Essay on Population* in his discussion of the difference between the positive and the preventive check, and which he went on to examine much more fully in later writing.

Since this is an issue which involves many complexities if treated exhaustively, I shall refer only to one illustration of its importance and I shall simplify outrageously in doing so. I choose it because of its potential importance in relation to the understanding of the profound changes which we have, perhaps unfortunately, come to label the industrial revolution, an event or set of linked changes which has radically altered almost every aspect of society and economy in the past two centuries. Since England was the scene on which the most significant elements of the change were first played out, the preceding centuries in English history hold a particular importance.

My example relates to the institution of marriage. In China, India, the Muslim world, the classical world of Greece and Rome, and indeed in much of Europe, but not in England and some other parts of western Europe for at least half a millennium before Malthus's day, the timing of marriage for women was determined by the process of physiological maturation. By convention it was almost impossible for a woman to be sexually adult and not married unless conspicuously handicapped mentally or physically. In contrast, in England both the timing and extent of marriage was determined by economic circumstances. As a result many women never married and those who married did so in their mid-twenties rather than their mid or later teens. The proximate reason for the English marriage pattern was that custom frowned on two married couples sharing the same household, and therefore to marry involved commanding the resources to establish a new, separate household. Lacking the resources to do this meant being unable to marry. Marriage came comparatively late in life and for many young people of both sexes might never occur at all. Moreover, it was sensitive to economic signals. In deteriorating economic circumstances marriage in the mass of the population was further postponed and the possibility that it might never take place was enhanced.[4]

To explore the background to this very unusual feature of English early modern society is outside the scope of this essay, but one consequence of its existence must be stressed. In a society in which marriage was universal and early, fertility was apt to be high and invariant, which in turn meant both that mortality would be equally high, since population growth must arrest at some point, and also that living standards would be low, the situation depicted in Figure 2. The population would be hard pressed to do more than survive and could expect few of the comforts of life. In a population in which fertility was

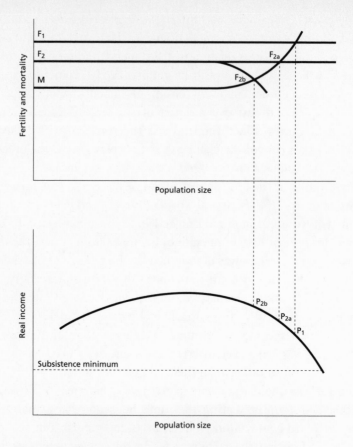

Figure 2: Fertility, mortality and living standards

much lower because of late marriage and also sensitive to economic influences, it is not difficult to show that there is a far greater likelihood that a substantial proportion of the population could live in comparatively comfortable circumstances.

Figure 2 illustrates this point, contrasting the 'high-pressure' (that is, high fertility and high mortality) case with a 'low-pressure' situation (that is, a situation where mortality is not forced up to a high level because fertility is responsive to the increasing pressure on resources). The two possibilities are shown by lines F_1 and F_{2b} in the figure. Note that where late marriage results in a lower level of fertility the point at which population growth will cease is significantly below the comparable case with early marriage and high fertility, even if fertility does not fall in response to the increasing pressure of numbers (line F_{2a} in Figure 2). The lower half of the figure shows the implications of the three contrasting cases for living standards. The potential advantages of low fertility are clear. The 'low-pressure' situation represented by F_{2b} might, for example, be found in a society in which the marriage system was capable of reading the 'signals' given by economic circumstances. If in deteriorating circumstances marriages were customarily delayed to a later age, or more men and women remained unmarried permanently, or both, fertility would be responsive to secular change in the economy and population growth would be arrested at an earlier stage than would be the case where marriage remained early and universal even when economic prospects darkened. In the former case population growth might cease while living standards were still tolerable: in the latter case the less fortunate elements in the population might teeter on the edge of a Malthusian precipice, periodically experiencing the kinds of disasters from famine and disease to which Malthus referred in his more apocalyptic moods.

Nothing is ever as straightforward as simple models might suggest. In many societies in which marriage was early and universal there were conventions and practices which restrained fertility to levels much lower than might have been expected. This was notably true of China, for example.[5] The village of Nakahara in Japan provides a particularly striking example of the same point. In Nakahara in the seventeenth and eighteenth centuries a combination of the practices of infanticide and adoption made it possible for individual couples to tailor both the size and the sex composition of their families to their wishes with surprising facility.[6] It is not clear how widespread such practices were in early modern Japan, but the example of Nakahara demonstrates that early and universal marriage is not necessarily synonymous either with high or invariant fertility levels. Equally, the mere existence of a west European type of marriage system did not ensure that subsistence crises and other concomitants of poverty and misery were avoided. The point is not that one set of marriage conventions invariably resulted in depressed living standards and the other in better prospects, but that Malthus's work suggested a range of questions which it is necessary and profitable to address in seeking to lay bare those structures and practices in agricultural societies which affected their capacities for economic growth.

For example, it is clearly possible for a society with marriage conventions of the type which prevailed in early modern England to have, as a result of this mode of reproduction, a very different structure of aggregate demand from that which will prevail in a society pressed into poverty by the nature of its marriage regime. If almost all available income must be devoted to the necessities of life, the structure of aggregate demand is not likely to be conducive to the development of secondary industry. In contrast, where a significant proportion of the income of a large fraction of the population enables them to look beyond their basic needs, a different range of possibilities exists. The marriage conventions found in early modern England are clearly not a sufficient cause of the industrial revolution. It may not even be possible to demonstrate conclusively that they were a necessary cause, but their significance in this context should not be understated.

So much for the relevance of Malthusian concepts to the understanding of pre-industrial societies. What changed with the industrial revolution to make the analytical framework developed by Malthus largely irrelevant? The answer is not far to seek. First, the industrial revolution removed the fundamental tension which affected all previous human societies. It had always previously been true that the maximum rate at which an economy could be induced to grow (that is, the maximum rate at which the ability to support additional population could rise) was well short of the rate at which population could increase. The contrast between arithmetic and geometric progression with which Malthus made such play in the first edition of the *Essay on Population* did not always capture pre-industrial reality accurately. Rates of growth of productive potential did not always decline (as implied by an arithmetic progression), but his insight was nonetheless fundamentally sound. Productive potential was handsomely outstripped by reproductive potential. There is reasonably good evidence, for example, that the underlying rate of growth of the English economy in the seventeenth and eighteenth centuries was about 0.5 per cent per annum on average.[7] The early modern English economy was an exceptionally successful one. No long-settled area grew at such a rate other than briefly in pre-industrial circumstances. A rate of growth of 0.5 per cent per annum, after all, implies a doubling in a little under 140 years and would mean a twelvefold growth in 500 years. However, after the industrial revolution the old verities in this connection were overturned with a vengeance. Even the staider economies have demonstrated a capacity to grow at 1.5 to 2.0 per cent per annum, and in recent decades many national economies have grown for decades at a time at a rate exceeding 5.0 per cent per annum. At such growth rates it is easily possible to eat your cake and have it, to accommodate relatively high rates of population growth while enjoying rising rather than falling living standards.

But this was not all. It had been regarded as a truism by most writers who interested themselves in the issue in the eighteenth century that rising prosperity would provoke more rapid population growth. Adam Smith, for example, made explicit his assumption that, in an era of greater prosperity and higher real wages, a combination of reduced mortality, brought about by better nutrition, and enhanced fertility, brought about by earlier and more universal marriage, would cause population growth to accelerate. As he put it, a higher demand for labour, like a higher demand for any other commodity, would result in a larger supply (admittedly with some time lag).[8] Rising prosperity in the world created by the industrial revolution did indeed result in lower mortality, though the benefit was often slow to appear and uncertain in its incidence. For a time in most countries growth rates rose, but soon declined because fertility fell thereafter even more markedly. Initially, the fall took place without the benefit of cheap and reliable mechanical or chemical means of preventing conception, but was later reinforced when, as today, the practice of sex can readily be divorced completely from the possibility of impregnation. With the sole exception of Iceland and Albania, there are today in Europe no countries in which fertility is sufficiently high to ensure that the next generation will be as large as the present generation. And there are many large countries, such as Germany, Italy and Russia, where fertility is now so low that each successive generation, if present fertility levels persist, will be only about two-thirds the size of its predecessor.

The links between production and reproduction which had been close and at times oppressive in agricultural societies, for reasons which were articulated with great effect by Malthus, have dissolved completely. Death, which once claimed young life as readily as old, is now almost the preserve of the elderly if one ignores violent death caused by road accidents, suicide and war, and the death from endogenous causes very early in life, and is prepared to make the bold assumptions that new afflictions like AIDS and the human form of BSE will not proliferate. Birth, which was once essential on a large scale generation by generation if populations were not to disappear, is now an optional event to a degree which would have amazed and might have horrified earlier generations, and is indulged in so rarely that, despite the huge reductions in mortality,[9] most western populations will soon begin to shrink fairly rapidly in the absence of any increase in the popularity of maternity. This does not mean, however, that reproduction has ceased to be an issue of great importance.

There is a sense, indeed, in which the old issues have not gone away. In the past fertility and mortality were in close balance and secular changes in population totals were slight and slow even though the vagaries of war, harvest and disease often produced very abrupt short-term changes. The two were kept in close balance by the forces which Malthus described. The carrying capacity of the land was limited. The capacity of population to increase greatly exceeded any possible growth in output. Production and reproduction were necessarily closely linked, even though differing social systems and environmental circumstances still allowed for striking contrasts between different societies in the way in which they coped with the tensions involved. At present, in the wake of the revolution in productive potential which we have labelled the industrial revolution and of the social and public health changes which have transformed fertility and mortality levels, population change can be much more dramatic. There are populations which have been doubling every 35 years or so for more than half a century.[10] At this rate a population would increase seven or eight times in a century. Yet there are also populations, both in Europe and in Asia, where current fertility levels suggest that in the absence of any substantial net migration, population will decline to only about one third of its current size within a century.[11] Neither trend can be long sustained without disaster. The former leads to nightmare scenarios with standing room only quite quickly. The latter means the disappearance of a population within a few centuries. In general countries where fertility has long been very high have entered a phase of rapid decline in the average number of children born to each couple. This is true of most countries in what used to be called the Third World, though not yet of sub-Saharan Africa. On the other hand, there is no current indication that fertility is likely to revive in countries where it is now very low; rather the reverse. Past experience suggests that forecasting in matters of this sort is largely idle. Parenthood may again become popular. But the notion that the disappearance of ancient tensions will lead to a general absence of difficulties is naïve and misguided.[12]

While it is debatable what the ideal size for any given population might be, it is nonetheless true that all societies need social mechanisms to restrain changes in population totals to modest amounts. Geometric growth operates as inexorably today as it did when Malthus wrote, and it operates as inexorably when growth is negative as when it is positive. On the assumption that both indefinite growth and indefinite decline are to be avoided, some social mechanism is needed to restrain over-rapid growth and to inhibit its opposite. Societies in the past evolved such mechanisms by trial and error, and in so doing have given historians fascinating topics to explore. It will be instructive to see how a problem which is at bottom the same as that faced by our forefathers is resolved, indeed whether it is resolved, though it may well be many years before the upshot is clear.

Notes and References

1 In the first *Essay on Population*, Malthus, having remarked in relation to mankind that 'No limits whatever are placed on the productions of the earth; they may increase for ever and be greater than any assignable quantity; yet still the power of population being a power of a superior order, the increase of the human species can only be kept commensurate to the increase of the means of subsistence, by the constant operation of the strong law of necessity acting as a check upon the greater power', then went on to claim 'Among plants and animals the view of the subject is simple. They are all impelled by a powerful instinct to the increase of their species; and this instinct is interrupted by no reasoning, or doubts about providing for their offspring. Wherever therefore there is liberty, the power of increase is exerted; and the superabundant effects are repressed afterwards by want of room and nourishment, which is

common to animals and plants; and among animals, by becoming the prey of others.' T.R. Malthus, *An Essay on the Principle of Population as it Affects the Future Improvement of Society* (London, 1798), in E.A. Wrigley and D. Souden (eds), *The Works of Thomas Robert Malthus*, vol. 1 (London, 1986), pp. 13–14. On the impact of Malthus's work on Darwin, see e.g. P.J. Bowler, 'Malthus, Darwin and the Concept of Struggle', *Journal of the History of Ideas*, 37 (1976), pp. 631–50: S. Herbert, 'Darwin, Malthus and selection', *Journal of the History of Biology*, 4 (1971), pp. 209–17.

2 See the fascinating investigation of this question in A.J.Coale, 'The Use of Modern Analytical Demography by T.R. Malthus', *Population Studies*, 33 (1979), pp. 329–32.

3 An excellent brief account of Malthus's work may be found in D. Winch, *Malthus* (Oxford, 1987). The most comprehensive account of his life and work is to be found in P. James, *Population Malthus: His Life and Times* (London, 1979). His writings as an economist are extensively described and analysed in S. Hollander, *The Economics of Thomas Robert Malthus* (Toronto, 1997).

4 The classic discussion of this issue, which initiated a very large literature on the subject, appeared in 1965: J. Hajnal, 'European Marriage Patterns in Perspective', in D.V. Glass and D.E.C. Eversley (eds), *Population in History: Essays in Historical Demography* (London, 1965), pp. 101–43.

5 J.Z. Lee and Wang Feng, *One Quarter of Humanity: Malthusian Mythology and Chinese Realities, 1700–2000* (Cambridge, Mass., 1999): Zhongwei Zhao, 'Deliberate Birth Control in China before 1970', *Population and Development Review*, 23 (1997), pp. 729–67.

6 T.C. Smith, *Nakahara: Family Farming and Population in a Japanese Village, 1717–1830* (Stanford, 1977), esp. ch. 5.

7 E.A. Wrigley and R.S. Schofield, *The Population History of England 1541–1871: A Reconstruction* (London, 1981), pp. 407–12.

8 '. . . the demand for men, like that for any other commodity, necessarily regulates the production of men; quickens it when it goes on too slowly, and stops it when it advances too fast.' A. Smith, *An Inquiry into the Nature and Causes of the Wealth of Nations*, ed. E. Cannan, 5th edn., 2 vols (London, 1961), I, p. 89, and more generally, ch. 8.

9 More than 95 per cent of all newborn children will pass their 50th birthdays at current age-specific mortality rates.

10 For example, in Africa, which has the largest number of such countries, this is true of Egypt, Nigeria, Kenya, Algeria, Morocco and South Africa among the countries with large populations.

11 Among the larger countries of Europe this is true of Germany, Italy, Spain and Russia, and in Asia of Japan.

12 As an example of the scale of the changes which may be in prospect, see
P. McDonald and R. Kippen, 'Labour Supply Prospects in 16 Developed
Countries, 2000–2050', *Population and Development Review*, 27 (2001), pp.
1–32. The authors discuss the implications of current demographic trends
for the future size of the labour force in a range of countries both in
Europe and Asia.

CLIVE TREBILCOCK

Surfing the Wave:
The Long Cycle in the
Industrial Centuries

Long-cycle theory presents one of the central mysteries of economic history. It proposes the notion that the global industrial economy – however much of the globe it has covered – has fluctuated from its earliest inception to an identifiable and protracted rhythm. As the second millennium drew to its close, the subject was revisited by a notable concentration of research, perhaps naturally seeking to pinpoint where the start of a new era in the human measurement of time intersected with the swing of the industrial long wave and the variation in human prosperity which it controls.

It seemed, too, as we made our uncertain way through the 1990s, that the long cycle might offer an optimistic perspective for the millennial turning-point. In the Blairite fairground which provides the symbols for the current economy – the fairground of the Dome and the Eye – why should the economic historians not have their speciality ride, the Big Dipper of the Market Place? The equipment indeed exists, is in good working order and is presently generating some interesting effects. This equipment offers an optimistic perspective because, of course, dippers go up as well as down.

The Big Dipper of Economic History may be demonstrated in a modern form by Figure 1 (see page 68). The diagram suggests that the long-run development of the industrial era may be represented by a series of waves or surges of economic growth, and that the period which straddles the end of the second and the beginning of the third millennium may provide the location for a new upsurge. It is not necessary to accept the implication in the graph that the pace of the waves is accelerating; there would be more, if by no means universal, consensus among analysts of economic growth in the long run about the general shape of the wave pattern.[1] A more orthodox shape for this pattern of waves is displayed in the data for the growth of world trade in Figure 2 (see page 70).

References to long waves or cycles in the process of growth occur in the publications of a varied group of academic economists including Aftalion, Jevons, Lenoir, Pareto and Spiethoff, as well as the Marxists Parvus and van Gelderen, and can be traced, in the writings of some minor British commentators, back as far as the 1840s. However, the really major insights were produced during the economic depression of the interwar years by the great Russian economist Nicolai Kondratieff (1892–1938) – who in 1925 postulated a fifty-year-long cycle in the performance of the world economy – and the equally eminent Viennese economic historian Joseph Schumpeter (1883–1950) – who generated much of the empirical evidence for Kondratieff's proposal.[2] Their work is well known, but interest in it has revived around the turn of the millennium, due, among other influences, to the first, astonishingly long-delayed, publication of Kondratieff's collected writings in 1998[3] and the sense, perceptible among the more informed economic journalism of recent times, that a long downswing may be coming to an end and that a new generation of innovations may be in the making.[4] It may also be possible, of course, that the turnings of millennia do tend to attune the collective consciousness towards long-term processes.

The cycle that Kondratieff believed he had detected displayed an upswing of 20–30 years and a downswing of a similar length, summing to a total of 50 years overall, for both upswing and downswing. Theoretically, the whole of industrial history since Britain's pioneering take-off in the eighteenth century could be described in this wave-like pattern. Ironically, as their critics pointed out, Kondratieff and Schumpeter in the 1920s and 1930s did not have enough industrial time, or cycles, for this pattern to establish a convincing completeness; they were stuck about half-way through the third wave. Even Schumpeter felt that historical circumstances fitted

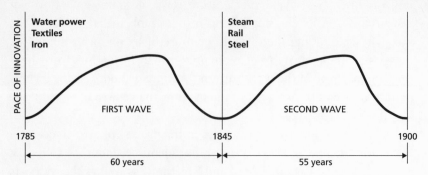

Figure 1: Surf's up – Schumpeter's waves accelerate (Source: *The Economist*, 20 February 1999, Survey, p. 8)

his three-cycle schema better than his theoretical analysis could explain. Now, of course, we have rather more time and more cycles against which the pattern can be tested.

Kondratieff's original proposition did not strive for excessive precision, 'he did not imagine that he had identified a long-time cycle which had an invariable period, or recurred in an unchanging way'.[5] There is a sensible flexibility in the length of the upswing and downswing and the turning-points between them. Indicators of price movements, interest rates and business activity established only a 'high probability' of a flow and ebb pattern in which the wave phases each lasted 'about' 20–30 years. Kondratieff did not attempt a theoretical explanation of the causes of the swings but defined four 'attendant conditions': significant changes in technology following major inventions; wars and social upheavals; the recruitment of new economies to the league of industrial countries; and gold discoveries. The last, in a world which no longer looks to precious metals to underpin monetary systems, has lost the force that it possessed in Kondratieff's day; but the other factors retain potency. Later, in his last months of freedom before incarceration by Stalin's thugs, he returned to the theme of technology change, theorizing that the long swings might reflect spurts in the reinvestment of fixed capital (since new bursts of investment might be convincingly associated with new waves of innovations).[6] But again a commonsensical latitude was

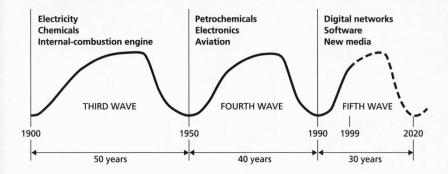

allowed in the link between technical change and the surge of the wave, 'For approximately two decades before the start of the rising wave long cycle, a revival of technical innovations is observed. Before and at the start of the rising wave broad application of these inventions to industrial practice is observed.'

Economists, no less than historians, examine their subject through the prism that is formed by the circumstances and problems of their own times. For Schumpeter, the challenge was to counter the allegation that the engine of capitalism was running down, destined for the culmination of stagnation. The wave or cycle was a useful device of refutation. His riposte was forthright: 'Capitalism . . . is by nature a form or method of economic change and not only never is, but never can be, stationary.'[7] His major work was concerned with the forces which caused capitalism to move away from equilibrium and he found the strongest force in the process of technological innovation. Business cycles happen because equilibrium is destroyed by innovations. Three types of cycle co-existed. The shortest pulse of the cycle (or Kitchin cycle) was caused merely by the accumulation and decumulation of inventories over a period of about three years. A medium cycle of around ten years (the Juglar cycle) was linked to individual innovations such as new textile machines, electric motors, radios, and, we could add, more recently, jet engines, computers or video recorders. The long cycle, named for Kondratieff, was

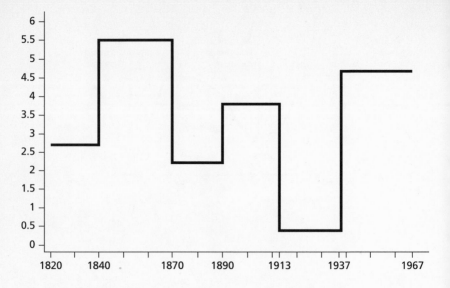

Figure 2: Annual compound rate of growth in world trade,
1820–1967 (constant prices)

generated by major innovations of the scale of railways, electrification, or, again more recently, global air transport or the IT revolution, which could not be completed within the span of a single Juglar. The upswing of the long cycle was distinguished by the occurrence of a 'cluster' of key innovations.

Innovation clusters occur precisely because they represent the lagged application of technological initiatives accumulated during Kondratieff's preceding 'revival' period; these must await the intersection of the technological vector with the appropriate market, investment and profit conditions before proceeding to the level of 'broad application'. They represent a form of stored economic energy. Further activity then ensues as innovations within a cluster prove mutually interactive and supportive.

If we combine the characteristics identified by Kondratieff and Schumpeter, we might expect each major new wave to be associated with three features: a surge in world manufacturing output; the industrialization of new economies; and a cluster of new innovations which provides the motive power.

The engine which drives the Big Dipper is clearly industrialization, and it starts cranking up during the acceleration of the world's first industrial nation in the eighteenth century. But there are those who have argued for longer antecedents of the process. One major Cambridge economic historian proposed, long before he came to Cambridge, that there was not a single industrial revolution commencing in Britain in the eighteenth century but a sequence of industrial revolutions stretching far further back in time.[8] Donald Coleman conceded that the British experience of 1750 onwards constituted the first industrial revolution to operate on the scale of the national economy.

But he found industrial revolutions, set at a smaller scale, much earlier: one in a single industry, the English woollen industry of the thirteenth and fourteenth centuries, involving large investment and major plant; another in a single sector of the English economy – the heat-using or coal-burning sector in the century 1540–1640 – again requiring heavy capital. In this second case, coal use in industries like cannon-making, iron-smelting, brewing, paper-making, sugar-refining and alum-making, rose by a factor of six over a 100-year span.

For Coleman, the sequence of industrial revolution proceeded from industrial through sectoral to national scale. The pattern was a 'sort of family of successive logistic curves' strewn across time and, again, centred on key innovations. Another broad wave pattern could thus be projected back to 1300 and beyond. Before the Big Dipper, there had been a Little Dipper.

The central supports of both structures were provided by industrialization. This involves the use of capital investment, machinery and human labour and skill to create factory production; it is emphatically not a craft-based or traditional handicraft mode of production. Even the thirteenth-century revolution in the woollen textile industry was based on the fulling-mill, a genuine factory of scale and cost. And the heat-users of the second revolution were among the largest industrial installations of their day. Nor, in the period in which the predecessor revolutions are located, was large-scale factory production confined to Britain. Well before the eighteenth century, comparable scales of output could be found in Bohemian or Austrian textiles, Italian silk or Catalan cotton.

So, even in the era of the Little Dipper, the emphasis falls not upon the traditional cottage industries of proto-industrialization – the somewhat questionable concept which some historians have invented to fill the chronological gap between feudalism and capitalism – but on the innovation-based sectors which brought new technology to manufacturing of scale and scope.[9]

Technological innovation has been with us for a long time and has affected the rhythm of economic life for centuries. Has it proved good for humankind? An optimist would argue that factory industrialization has proved the greatest generator of wealth known to history. True, he would hope that new technology would find a way of protecting the ozone layer before older technology finally succeeds in puncturing it. And, of course, it is true, and powerfully argued by some of more pessimistic inclination, that industrialization has created inequalities, that it has made some individuals, some classes, and some nations, disproportionately richer, inequitably faster than others.

The last point contains truth, but it is not a static truth. Over time, more economic benefits have accrued to a greater proportion of the community, both national and international. Even if some wealth remains disproportionate, the average level of wealth continues to rise in virtually all sectors of the industrial world. There are frictions and dysfunctions and omissions, and some of these are large – in primary-producing areas of the globe, up to continental scale – but the record of the industrial centuries suggests that the long-term pressures are towards a greater prosperity which is more widely – if not satisfactorily – distributed. And that, of course, leaves aside the *reductio ad absurdum* argument: what is, or was, the alternative generator of more widespread prosperity?

Table 1 shows the performance of Gross Domestic Product per head for five countries – admittedly they are advanced, but equally they have *become* advanced in the modern era – over a period of some 120 years. The data reveal that, in real terms, the average Briton had an income in 1989 five times greater than in 1870, the average American and Frenchman eight times greater, the average German ten times greater and the average Japanese twenty-four times greater. In 1870, Japan was by far the most agricultural of this sample, almost entirely reliant upon primary production. No doubt, it is reprehensible that some of these societies did better than others, but surely beneficial that all did better, much better, than before.

Table 1: GDP per capita ($ in 1985 relative prices)

	1870	1890	1913	1950	1973	1989
UK	2,610	3,383	4,024	5,651	10,063	13,468
USA	2,247	3,101	4,854	8,611	14,103	18,317
France	1,571	1,995	2,734	4,149	10,323	13,387
Germany	1,300	1,660	2,606	3,339	10,110	13,989
Japan	618	842	1,114	1,563	9,237	15,101

But, over the industrial centuries, this process of advance was not linear. Our protagonists, the thinkers at the centre of this essay, contend that the advance ran in waves.

They by no means command universal applause. Some economic opinion has little truck with the notion of long cycles and rejects the notion of pattern in the maelstrom of growth.[10] Some economists acknowledge a broad underlying current within the system but contend that it also contains too much 'noise' or 'interference', too many counter-currents for the swell to etch any clear pattern in the sand. Others still argue that there is more noise than system, more chaos than current.[11]

From the first industrial revolution to about the present day, the advocates of the long cycle would argue that there have been four Kondratieff long waves, perhaps coming on five. What then does the historical record suggest, or how can it be arranged?

The first of the long waves is conventionally dated at about 1790–1840. The new industrial revolutions in the upswing 1790–1820 were those of Britain and Belgium. The cluster of innovations came in cotton textiles, steam-power and ironmaking. There was clearly a surge in world industrial output. The subsequent downswing, 1820–40, was composed of the economic disruption and deflation in Europe which followed the end of the French Revolutionary and Napoleonic Wars.

The second cresting wave is often called the Railway Kondratieff and was driven by the huge upsurge in rail construction within Great Britain and Continental Europe between 1840 and 1870. This rail expansion dragged in its wake the key heavy industrial sectors of steel and mechnical engineering. These made up the cluster of innovations. The new industrial revolutions of this era were provided by the economic take-offs of France, the German states and the United States. There was another clear surge in world industrial output. The downswing of the Second Kondratieff came with the depression in prices and profits – another deflationary phase – and the rise of international industrial competition which economic historians call the First Great Depression and allot to it the cyclical turning-point years 1873 for the onset and 1896 for the culmination. In length, falling between the 1840s and the mid 1890s, it would not look very different from the first long cycle of 1790 to 1840.

The third upswing started around 1896 and ran nearly twenty years until 1914. This was the high-technology Kondratieff, characterized by major breakthroughs in chemicals, dyestuffs, electrical engineering, mass production and the first automobiles. The new industrial revolutions of this era included the take-offs of Japan, Italy, Sweden and major acceleration in Russia and Austria, as well as renewed activity in France, Germany and the USA, if less so in Britain. Again, this was more than enough to produce a surge in world industrial output, which is clearly visible on the curve of world economic growth (see Figure 3; and Figure 2 for the performance of world trade).

All of the new technology from this innovation cluster was heavily applied in the First World War, of course, and it much influenced the nature of that conflict.[12] War and its aftermath provided the turning-point and the economic effects of war undoubtedly deepened the downswing to produce another Great Depression of the international economy – strictly the second – occupying the interwar years 1919–39, with the Great Crash of 1929–32 at its centre. War again provided a break-point which ended this cycle. If the start and culmination dates of this cycle are taken as roughly 1896–1945, this long cycle again seems about the same shape and length of its predecessors.

Kondratieff's intuition that wars are in some way related to the long

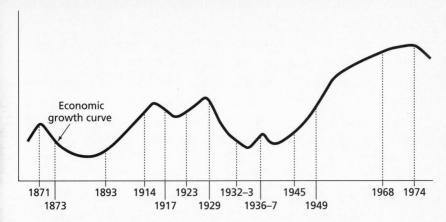

Figure 3: Long waves in economic growth (Source: drawn from Figure 3 of Mandel, *op. cit.*, p. 39)

cycle appears to be borne out. Wars have been associated with all four of the Kondratieff long waves fully experienced to date. This may not be surprising. However, the wars are not randomly distributed through the long cycle. Rather, they tend to fall within the upswing or at turning-points. The upswing of the First Kondratieff contained the French Wars (1793–1815); that of the Second Kondratieff, the Crimean War (1853–56); that of the Third Kondratieff, the Sino-Japanese, Spanish-American, Boer and Russo-Japanese Wars (all within the period 1894–1905); that of the Fourth Kondratieff was immediately prefaced by the Second World War. The Franco-Prussian (1870–1), First and Second World Wars all fell at, and clearly impacted upon, important turning-points in the cycle. Victory over France in 1871 helped produce an over-speculation crisis in Germany which halted even the industrial charge of the German states; the dire consequences for world trade and international capital flows of the First World War are too well known to need reiteration; yet the technological advances and appetite for international economic understanding generated by the Second World War helped promote the capital upswing of the Fourth Kondratieff.

The two world wars are clearly major examples of vast displacements to world civilization which could not but exert global economic pressures; yet they stand at diametrically opposed points on the cycle: one formed the introduction to a severe downswing in the interwar years, the other to a strong upswing after 1945 which contained a record-breaking investment boom.

It may be doubted whether some of these wars (the Crimean, Spanish-American or Boer) have created sufficient displacement to exercise any significant economic impact; though the economic effects of the last of these have usually been underrated.[13] On the other hand, the wars fought by Japan in the 1890s and 1900s had strong and positive effects on the early industrialization of this maritime economy.[14]

The associations between long-cycle upswings and wars must necessarily be highly complex and the reverse of transparent. Here, it is not possible to do more than hint at some possible linkages; but these obviously require more rigorous exploration. It is possible, even likely, that innovation clusters may alter the military balance between strategies of offence and defence, or the balance of (fire) power between individual nation-states. Or it is possible that upswings generate additions to state revenues which in turn make higher levels of military expenditure sustainable. On the other hand, the causation could run in the opposite direction (or in both). The opposite direction could involve high levels of military demand which provide a dependable market for innovational capital goods technologies.[15] Or high levels of military research and development may generate streams of scientific discoveries which produce technological breakthroughs that, in turn, are 'spun off' into the non-military industrial sector and there help feed a Schumpeterian cluster of innovations.[16] In downswings, it would be nice to think, there are insufficient resources or new ideas with which to fight. It takes deliberate and focused rearmament (less the economic consequences of Mr Keynes, than the economic consequences of Herr Hitler) to reverse this conjunction.

The experience of war and the experience of economic change are often taken to be profoundly, if vaguely, associated. The vagueness follows from the fact that, historically, economists have paid insufficient attention to war, treating it, in the long liberal economic tradition, as an inconvenient aberration, an interruption to the normal rational process of the market, rather than as an integral part of international behaviour. This is strange, considering how much time in the modern era nations have spent expanding and disrupting their markets by fighting one another. The empirical evidence suggests that Kondratieff was on to something, if not quite on to what.

The remaining issue is how well – three-quarters of a century after Kondratieff and nearly a half-century after Schumpeter – the empirical evidence continues to fit the wave hypothesis. To the ear of the economic historian, perhaps attuned – or wishing to be attuned – to long-run modes of description, the sound of the surf still has a rhythm to it.

That rhythm appears to resume in, or before, 1945. Thanks to Whittle's jet engine,[17] and thanks to the wartime development of radar, and the decoding computers of Bletchley Park, it could be claimed that the makings of the next innovational cluster were already in place by the end of the Second World War. They were fully applied in the ensuing 'Golden Age' in the form of mainframe computers, jet-powered civil aviation, and petro-chemicals. This Golden Age saw spectacular growth in reconstructed older economies such as Italy, West Germany, and Japan, all of which experienced 'economic miracles' in this period. The expansion of the world economic growth curve 1945–73 (see Figure 3; and Figure 2 for the impact on world trade) was huge and required a phenomenal amount of investment to pay for it; levels of capital formation which had previously counted as record peaks became decade-long norms. Two economies, Japan and Norway, came close to investing an extraordinary 40 per cent of national income, probably the highest levels known to economic history.[18]

This remarkable growth was supported by a specific production structure. It involved the mass production of standardized products, oligopolistic competition between vertically integrated large corporations, and the active promotion of cheap products in a mass consumer market.[19] However, it may turn out that this version of efficiency was attached to one specific long cycle and that other definitions may be needed in subsequent cycles.

War was not an absent influence in this cyclical upswing. Japan's 'miraculous' growth – which reached 12 per cent per annum advance in GNP at its fastest – was kick-started by military demand from US forces in Korea. Secondly, the high levels of US military expenditure necessary for the maintenance of Pax Americana involved a concentration upon scientific research and development which, some economists believe, 'spun off' an unusual stream of technological innovations into the US home economy and helped swell the current cluster.[20]

However, few new industrial take-offs were evident in the upswing of the Fourth Kondratieff, although the South Korean Five Year Development Plan of 1962–7 gave some indication of what was to come from that economy, and the emergence of Brazil as an industrial force offered some additional support. The East Asian NICs (Newly Industrializing Countries) began their growth surge within the upswing of the Fourth Kondratieff, but then fell out of synchroniza-, tion with the world trend; they continued to expand into the 1980s and encountered a lagged downturn only in the 1990s. South Korea, by the late 1970s, possessed the world's largest plants in the textile, plywood, shipbuilding, cement, and heavy machinery industries. But this did not really fit the larger pattern of world development (see below). The count and chronology of fresh industrial revolutions aside, the upswing of the Fourth Kondratieff emerges as a fairly powerful example of its kind.

About the turning-point of this long cycle there can be little doubt. It is scored into the economic record of the twentieth century with diamond clarity. The oil shock of 1973 – which quadrupled the price of crude – reinforced by its lesser cousin of 1977, slammed the brakes on the global economy (perhaps already slowing) and turned much of the western world into a petrol station queue. The world's biggest economies rocked in the after-shocks throughout the 1970s, with only Japan – now reduced to a mere 4 per cent growth in GNP per annum (1973–9) – demonstrating, by deft application of fuel-economizing technology, any quick-footedness or resilience. Rates of growth of national product, productivity and wages slowed in all the large economies. Unemployment rates and inflation rose in curious symmetry to produce the unattractive phenomenon of 'stagflation'. Previous downswings had been deflationary; it was the special contribution of the post-Keynesian world[21] to achieve the difficult combination of inflation and stagnation. If mass unemployment and shrinkage in world trade were the hallmarks of the interwar downswing, stagflation was the dominant feature of the 1970s, the first phase of the postwar downswing.

Inflation abated in the 1980s, but the rest of the economic record remained, at best, mixed. The gas-guzzling USA continued to languish, apparently suffering the post-industrial maturity which had afflicted Britain a century earlier, as well as the misjudgements of Reagonomics. Britain itself underwent Mrs Thatcher, a dose of 'market realism' and a burst of improved productivity which looks increasingly like a blip on the long-term trend. Japan, with her impetus already much reduced, and under disastrous policy guidance, went into the 'bubble economy' speculation of the late 1980s, and came out, under still more disastrous policy guidance, in the early 1990s with low, and by the later 1990s, negative growth rates. For Japan the 1990s comprised the 'lost decade'.

Meanwhile, what had been the world's second biggest economy, that of the USSR, fell to pieces, and into de-industrialization. Even the 'little tiger' economies of Asia, apparently paddling fast against the downswing of the wave, missed their stroke in 1997 and were left floundering, after scarcely two decades or so of imitating Japan.

The downswing of the fourth wave, then, looks all too real. If the Kondratieff chronology continues to run true, it should draw to a close some 25–30 years after the turning-point of the early 1970s, that is, in the late 1990s, or early 2000s. Indeed, some, perhaps surprisingly many, observers have already claimed to detect the harbingers, or, less plausibly, even the components, of the Fifth Kondratieff upswing.

Intriguingly, academics and journalists start rediscovering Kondratieff only when an upswing is sensed to be nigh; he is unaccountably less popular at the beginning of a downswing. Of course, historians are emphatically debarred from the business of prediction. But the conjunction of a new upswing with the approach of a new millennium poses a temptation difficult to resist. Some have not resisted. In the 1980s and 1990s, several analysts went in search of Kondratieff straws in the wind, or disturbed sand in the shallows. In 1982, Jonathan Steinberg published a prescient think-piece on the end of the Fourth Kondratieff downswing in the *Financial Times*; in 1998 William Rees-Mogg – who was instrumental in achieving the publication of the collected works – featured Kondratieff in a major appraisal in *The Times*; and the idea of the accelerated wave surfaced in the *Economist* essay of February 1999.[22] Probably well in advance of its arrival, there is already an academic debate concerning the appropriate production structure for the upswing of the Fifth Kondratieff.[23]

The accelerated wave will not wash. This form of prediction falls down on several counts. For one thing, it disregards Kondratieff's own insistence that it is unwise to date end-points of cycles with excessive precision; this is a warning that should be heeded. For another, it seems clear that the turning-points of the Third Kondratieff (upswing *c*. 1895–1914; downswing *c*. 1919–45) and Fourth Kondratieff (upswing *c*. 1945–73; downswing *c*. 1973–2000?) have fallen more or less where Kondratieff and Schumpeter might have expected to find them. Thirdly, there is the problem that historical processes become notoriously more difficult to decipher as they press closer to the present. To distinguish the tree from the wood, the ripple from the preceding wave, is a perilous undertaking in such circumstances. Surrounded by the innovations of the last few years, it would be rash indeed to conclude that these are already the very same innovations that will power the next upswing. We would do well to recall Kondratieff's own observation that, 'for approximately two decades *before* the start of a rising wave long cycle, a revival of technical innovations is observed'.[24]

It is particularly disturbing that the accelerated wave hypothesis relies entirely upon the variable of innovation. This was a major driver but by no means the only driver of the Kondratieff–Schumpeter waves. True upwings require also a new upsurge in world industrial output and a spate of new industrial revolutions. If the USA found a remarkable source of renewed productivity and output growth in the 1990s – and apparently slipped the leash of post-industrial maturity in the process – it is equally striking that the world's formerly second and third largest economies suffered marked deceleration for the best part of the decade. And where are the new industrial revolutions? Are the little tigers going to revive and produce them? If so, they have not managed it yet. Or will the new industrial revolutions, when they arrive, come from quite other directions? From India? From Turkey? From China?

But, even if the focus is returned to innovation, the technological evidence surely suggests that a Schumpeterian cluster is in the offing, rather than with us already.

Interestingly, Ernest Mandel, writing in 1995, as a sceptic about the possibilities of a new long-wave 'recovery', and as a Marxist inclined to detect the symptoms of capitalism's eventual stagnation, could imagine as potential constituents of a fresh innovation surge only 'billions of "ecologically clean" motor cars . . . billions of household or laser application robots' and did not think them 'likely to be sold in the foreseeable future', although he did concede the possible importance of 'new advances in biotechnology'.[25] Mandel had predicted accurately the onset of the downswing of the Fourth Kondratieff but was not minded to recognize the arrival of the early gusts heralding the upswing of the Fifth.[26]

Perhaps the glass has cleared a little in the meantime, and the cluster in the offing has become rather more discernible. However, proper appreciation of current innovation prospects involves recognition not only of the science involved but of its limitations. Interactive communications and teaching systems are almost here – we should note that sending canned lectures down wires is not 'distance learning' – but still require much development. Responsive IT, which allows the user to do what he or she wants to do, will eventually replace 'advanced' software which gives the user a plethora of options and a poverty of useful choice. 'Fuzzy logic' systems which think more like humans – that is, fuzzily – are in the research departments of the big telecommunications specialists. So are 'virtual reality' methods of training and simulation. But they are not yet within the consumer's reach. E-commerce has made a start, but that is all it is; the world market place will come into the sitting rooms of the multitude, but this will take time. The internet is with us, but it has filled cyberspace with millions of 'volumes' of irrecoverable and illegible information; it is the biggest library of all time, but it lacks even a semi-efficient catalogue. In due course, the really intelligent search engines will come, and some of the research needed to develop them – in the areas, for example, of molecular and medical informatics – is under way. But, at present, the internet is just a steam engine; it is not even a train, let alone an intercontinental railway line. It is a symbol of a journey which has barely begun.

Another journey which has started will take the vital operations of medical treatment and drug development from the status of empirical to that of predictive processes. The main vehicle here is the Human

Genome Project – centred in the UK at the Sanger Institute at Hinxton, outside Cambridge – which will map the entire genetic structure of the human being.[27] The task is then to match particular gene sequences to particular disease patterns. SNP (Single Nucleotide Polymorphism) mapping of genetic data has already located the ApoE gene associated with Alzheimer's disease, and other matches have been found for psoriasis and Type 2 diabetes, and, it seems likely, for migraine. Similarly, the genetic code of the bacterium *Salmonella typhi*, which causes typhoid fever, has been cracked – in another international effort incorporating the Sanger Institute – and every target in the organism, at which drugs or vaccines could be directed, has become visible. In a separate research operation, the gene that controls cell division in cancer cells has been identified – winning Sir Paul Nurse of the Imperial Cancer Research Fund the Nobel Prize for Medicine – and gene P53 has been traced in half of all cancerous cells.

Once such molecular targets have been identified, high-throughput screening by computer can rapidly test the increased number and variety of molecules generated by modern high-throughput chemistry until the most effective drug candidate is found. The welding together of the disciplines of information technology and pharmaceutics could produce another locomotive of great power.[28]

Yet again care is needed. Mono-genetic diseases are rare: there are few single matches between individual genes and particular diseases. Many diseases, by contrast, are products of multiple gene conjunctions; it may take twenty or so conjoining genetic characteristics to create the disposition towards a specific disease. Identifying how these genes and their protein products interact to cause disease, and spotting which individual molecular target is amenable to modulation by drugs, is no simple matter. And the genetic influences are only part of the narrative of a particular disease; contextual and lifestyle variables are often necessary contributors to its unhappily unfolding story, and, without them, more happily, the story may not unfold.

Medical research in other areas also seems to be approaching key turning-points. If the ethical problems surrounding human cloning are resolved, as in the area of therapeutic cell culture they surely must be, the prospects for treatment by tissue transplantation are huge. By cloning embryonic stem cells which can then be directed to develop into any kind of tissue, from insulin-secreting cells, through nervous system tissue to heart tissue, doctors could be given an armoury of weapons at least as important as the first vaccines or the first antibiotics.

Nanotechnology, allied to medicine, has in sight the development of tiny machines which can be launched into the body to deliver treatment from within. These miniaturized vehicles, probably swallowed as pills, will act as micro-surgeons or micro-pharmacists with the ability to attack cancerous cells *in situ* or deliver drugs by nano-capsule precisely to the seat of infection or disease. For diagnostic purposes, it is planned to use a laboratory that can be ingested: a robot smaller than an aspirin will cruise the body measuring temperature, acidity, oxygen concentration and other key indicators in the locations which it passes and will transmit the results to monitors near the patient. Such devices are at the research stage. But nanotechnology can already supply highly sensitized strips or cards which are effectively micro-laboratories that can carry out chemical analysis of minute quantities of body fluids in seconds; this could, and almost certainly will, revolutionize the speed of diagnosis of any of the many conditions requiring the sampling of blood characteristics.

This generation of scientific and technological initiatives does not look random. There are common threads which bind them – often represented by the fibres, modems, memories and data-processing capacity of information technology – which suggest that they may have the binding power of a genuine cluster.

All of this, of course, is crystal-ball gazing, which historians are not supposed to do. But if not in the threshold months of a new millennium, when ever? If Kondratieff was right, we should enter the millennium on a rising crest, an upswinging new wave. Maybe it was not accidental that, in December 1999, the European Union issued its most optimistic economic forecast ever. Then in 2000 the stock markets tumbled and the dot.com ventures went into free fall. Just a cross current?[29]

Possibly the most powerful of all images of the wave is Hokusai's veritable *tsumani*, as it roars in on Kanagawa, with Mount Fuji visible below the crest. Kondratieff and Schumpeter bequeathed to us all the fun of working out just where we float on the economic equivalent of this monster.

Katsushika Hokusai, 'The Great Wave off Kanagawa' (*Metropolitan Museum of Art, New York*).

Notes and References

1 Agreement would probably most readily settle around a chronology which is loosely based on that suggested by Ernest Mandel, *Long Waves of Capitalist Development: A Marxist Interpretation* (Guildford, 1995), pp. 1–7, although it is not necessary to agree either with his theoretical positioning or his pessimism. This chronology features upswings of the long cycle in the periods: 1790–1825, 1848–73, 1894–1913, 1940 [48]–1967 [73]; and downswings in the periods: 1826–47, 1874–93, 1914–39, and 1968 [73]–? Excessive attachment to single years as turning-points is usually unwise. This pattern conforms broadly with that revealed by the growth rates in world trade shown in Figure 2.

2 The link between protracted economic downturn and long-cycle theory was not coincidental. One of Schumpeter's purposes in his key work *Business Cycles* (New York, 1939) was to divine the causes of the 1930s slump, and a possible way out of it. His own favoured chronology for the

long cycles (cf. note 1), within the timespan available to him, placed upswings in the periods: 1786–1813, 1843–69 and 1898–1913, while allotting Kondratieff 'recessions' to the phases: 1814–42, 1870–97 and 1919–39, although he too warned against an excess of exactitude in the quest for turning-points.

3 N. Kondratieff, *The Works of Nicolai Kondratieff*, 4 vols (London, 1998), ed. N. Makasheva, W.J. Samuels and V. Barnett. Kondratieff's writings had failed to circulate freely in Russia, not least because he was arrested on Stalin's orders in 1930 and executed in 1938. The first appearance in English of the long cycle that was to bear his name came in the essay 'Long Waves in Economic Life', *Review of Economic Statistics* (1935), 17, 2, pp. 105–15, itself a shortened translation of a section in Volume 1 of *Voprosy kon'iunktury* (1925).

4 *The Economist, ibid*; William Rees-Mogg, 'Living in the Long Run', *The Times*, 6 August 1998. It was Rees-Mogg's publishing house which published the collected works in 1998.

5 Quoted by Rees-Mogg, *ibid*.

6 *Dinimica tsen promoyshlennykh i sel'skokhoziaisvennykh tovarov* (Moscow, 1928).

7 *Capitalism, Socialism and Democracy* (London, 1942), p. 82. Schumpeter's stress in *Business Cycles* upon technological innovation as the vehicle of change has been reconfirmed by some influential later work. See Mahdavi, *Technological Innovation: An Efficiency Investigation* (Stockholm, 1972), and A. Kleinknecht, *Innovation Patterns in Crisis and Prosperity* (London, 1987). But the 'long depression' since 1968/73 has sparked a reworking of the Marxist concept of capitalistic stagnationism; see Mandel, *op.cit.*

8 D.C. Coleman, 'Industrial Growth and Industrial Revolutions', *Economica* (1956). Donald Coleman was successively Lecturer in Industrial History at the LSE from 1951, Professor of Economic History at the LSE 1969–71 and Professor of Economic History at Cambridge, 1971–81. In a rather grander scheme of things, Immanuel Wallerstein proposes a series of long waves which also stretches back far in time over 'very long temporality' to at least 1500. However, this proto-long-wave is powered by tension between 'the centre and the periphery' rather than by a technological dynamic. I. Wallerstein, 'A Brief Agenda for the Future of Long-Wave Research', in A. Kleinknecht, E. Mandel and I. Wallerstein (eds), *New Findings in Long Wave Research* (Basingstoke, 1992) and 'Long Waves as Capitalistic Processes', Paris Colloqium, *Research on Long Waves*, March 1993.

9 See the critique by D.C. Coleman, 'Proto-industrialisation: A Concept too Many', *Economic History Review*, 36 (1983), pp. 435–48; also,

S. Ogilvie and M. Cerman (eds), *European Proto-Industrialization* (Cambridge, 1996); and, for the originial proposals, P. Kriedte *et al.*, *Industrialization before Industrialization* (Cambridge, 1982), and F. Mendels, 'Proto-industrialization: The First Phase of the Industrialization Process', *Journal of Economic History* (1972).

10 George Garvy, for instance, argued that Kondratieff's waves were, at least in part, the result of the specific techniques of statistical analysis employed, and that the dating of many of the turning-points was arbitrary. G. Garvy, 'Kondratieff's Theory of Long Cycles', *Review of Economic Statistics* (1943), pp. 203–20. Now we can see that the last three turning-points are represented by the onset of the First World War, the culmination of the Second, and the oil shock of 1973, Garvy's point about arbitrariness may be thought to have lost some force. And see G. Imbert, *Des mouvements de longue durée Kondratieff* (Aix-en-Provence, 1956), U. Weinstock, *Das Problem der Kondratieff Zyklen* (Munich, 1964), C. Freeman (ed.), *Long Waves in the World Economy* (London, 1983), A. Tylecote, *The Long Wave in the World Economy* (London, 1992), and E. Mandel, *op. cit.* (1995). The latter, itself based on a famous series of Cambridge Marshall Lectures, seeks to correlate long waves in capitalistic growth with 'long waves of class struggle'.

11 Solomos Solomou, *Phases of Economic Growth 1850–1973: Kondratieff Waves and Kuznets Swings* (Cambridge, 1987), and *Economic Cycles: Long Cycles and Business Cycles since 1870* (Manchester, 1998). Solomou prefers the shorter Kuznets swing to the long cycles as the underlying pattern.

12 The rate of usage of ammunition in the First World War would have been impossible without mass production processes in the supply system, while the *machine*-gun, both in nomenclature and practice, provided a lethal link between industrial and military technologies.

13 See Clive Trebilcock, 'War and the failure of industrialization: 1899 and 1914', in J.M. Winter, *War and Economic Development* (Cambridge, 1975), pp. 139–64.

14 As the Korean War did on the re-industrialization of Japan after 1950, in the format of a heavy-industrial, high-technology economy. The US war machine now needed industrial support within the theatre of combat. Formerly, the policy of the US Government of Occupation had been to cast Japanese economic reconstruction in the form of agricultural and light industrial development. For the effect of war on early Japanese growth, see K. Yamamura, 'Success Ill-Gotten?: The Role of Meiji Militarism in Japanese Technological Progress', *Journal of Economic History*, 37 (1977); but, for a contrary view, see A.C. Kelley and J.G. Williamson, *Lessons from Japanese Development: An Analytical Economic History* (Chicago, 1974).

15 See N. Rosenberg, 'Capital Goods, Technology and Economic Growth', *Oxford Economic Papers*, new series, 15 (1963); also N. Rosenberg (ed.), *The American System of Manufactures* (Edinburgh, 1969), pp. 1–86, and N. Rosenberg and D.C. Mowery, *Technology and the Pursuit of Economic Growth* (Cambridge, 1989).

16 Clive Trebilcock, ' "Spin-off" in British Economic History: Armament and Industry, 1760–1914', *Economic History Review*, 22 (1969), pp. 474–90, and 'British Armaments and European Industrialization, 1890–1914', *Economic History Review*, 26 (1973), pp. 254–72.

17 The engine which powered Britain's first fully operational military aircraft, the Meteor.

18 Clive Trebilcock, 'Capital Formation in Europe, 1920–70', in C.M. Cipolla (ed.), *The Fontana Economic History of Europe: The Twentieth Century*, vol. 5, pt. 1 (Glasgow, 1982).

19 In two famous volumes, Al Chandler proposed the 'high-throughput' multi-divisional, large-scale corporation as a definition of business efficiency. It remains to be seen whether Chandler's insight is time-limited. A. Chandler, *Strategy and Structure* (Cambridge, Mass., 1962) and *Scale and Scope* (Cambridge, Mass., 1990); and see note 23 below.

20 E. Benoit and H. Lubell, in E. Benoit (ed.), *Disarmament and World Economic Interdependence* (Oslo, 1967), pp. 48–57; also L. Urban in *ibid.*, p. 164; and compare, for the UK, *Committee of Inquiry into the Aircraft Industry* (Plowden Committee), Cmnd 2853, p. 29, also ch. 14 and appendix K.

21 But not of Keynes: stagflation was at least partly the result of the *misapplication* of Keynesian policies, more exactly, the pursuit of full employment strategies, without the incomes policies which Keynes had defined as their essential counterparts.

22 J. Steinberg, 'Why the Recession May Last until 1996', *Financial Times*, 8 September 1982; *The Times*, loc. cit.; *Economist*, loc. cit. Mandel notes seven international colloquia on 'long waves' between 1985 and 1989, *op. cit.*, p. 116. There has also been a notable surge of academic publications on long waves in the last two decades, see fn 10 and Mandel, *op. cit.*, pp. 158ff.

23 See, for instance, A. Amin, *Post-Fordism: Models, Fantasies and Phantoms of Transition* (Oxford, 1994). The proposition is that the mass-consuming markets of the Fourth Kondratieff have become saturated and unstable and that a more flexible and agile production and regulation structure will be needed to handle the more individualistic consumer tastes which will be serviced by the technological innovations of the Fifth Kondratieff. This issue has prompted an extended technical discussion between

regulation theorists, neo–Schumpeterians and flexible production strategists. In this setting, it is a debate best alluded to, rather than entered.

24 My emphasis.

25 *Op. cit.*, p. 112.

26 E. Mandel, 'The Economics of Neo-Capitalism', *The Socialist Register*, 56 (1964).

27 On 27 December 1999, the scientific journal *Nature* published the first genetic map of a single chromosome, Chromosome 22. This was a product of the Sanger Institute. The deadline for the completion of the entire Human Genome Project is 2003, suggestive timing for a new Schumpeterian cluster. And see Matt Ridley, *Genome: The Autobiography of a Species* (London, 1999).

28 It is not transparent how this will be achieved outside the 'Fordist' or Chandlerian multi-divisional large corporations. It took governments and the biggest of US big business to map the Genome. True, smaller ventures are at the cutting edge in software development and biotechnology launches. But the big pharmaceutical companies have a close interest in the possibility of predictive drug development and the research budgets to pursue it.

29 Mandel would argue not. From his Marxist standpoint he refined an updated variant of the old doctrine of capitalistic stagnation which would have infuriated Schumpeter. In this scenario, the downswing of the Fourth Kondratieff becomes a 'long depression' which does not end. Capitalistic competition and worker resistance combine to snuff out business cycle upturns and return the system to recession, *op. cit.*, p. 138. The long wave is a far happier idea. Or at least it was until 11 September 2001.

JOHN A. THOMPSON

Americans and Their Century

We owe the phrase 'The American Century' to Henry Luce, the founder of Time-Life, who used it as the title of an essay in *Life* magazine in February 1941. 'Consider the twentieth century,' Luce wrote. 'It is ours not only in the sense that we happen to live in it but ours also because it is America's first century as a dominant power in the world.'[1] Usually thought of as bombastic, Luce's claim might well be judged too modest. Few now would question that the United States has been *the* dominant power in the world since 1945. It could well be argued that earlier in the century, too, the course of world politics was more affected by America's actions (and non-actions) than by those of any other country.

The United States was not only on the winning side in the three major geopolitical conflicts of the twentieth century – World War I, World War II and the Cold War – but was also decisive in the outcome of each. In World War I, the Allies had become dependent on American supplies and finance even before the US entered the war, but in the end the American military contribution also became vital. When, following the collapse of Russia, the Germans made their final thrust on the western front in 1918, it must be doubtful whether Foch would have been able to turn the tide without the rapidly increasing flow of fresh troops from across the Atlantic. In World War II, American forces were largely responsible for the defeat of Japan, and while, of course, the brunt of the land fighting against Germany was borne by the Russians, it was the more than eightfold increase in American armaments production between 1941 and 1943 that gave the Allies the tremendous superiority in *matériel* that carried them to victory on all fronts. By 1943, about 60 per cent of all the combat munitions of the Allies was being produced in the USA.[2] In the Cold War, the United States not only largely organized the effort to contain Soviet and Communist power but also provided the major part of the resources.

In more peaceful enterprises, too, the United States has played a leading role. No doubt, broader forces lay behind the development of the international organizations that have become such a prominent feature in world affairs, but as a matter of historical fact the League of Nations and the United Nations (and their associated agencies), the IMF, the World Bank, GATT, and, more recently, the WTO, have all been the products of American initiative and leadership. Whatever the economic importance of Marshall aid *per se*, it is hard to imagine the postwar recovery and integration of Western Europe without American assistance and encouragement, to say nothing of the confidence generated by the security guarantee institutionalized in NATO. The development of modern Japan, likewise, has been much affected by US policy, during the occupation and since. The American role has been crucial in the creation and survival of the state of Israel. And in many less dramatic and precise ways, the activities of the US government and its agents, and signals and rumours of what 'Washington' wants, have had a significant influence on the course of events in Latin America and other parts of the Third World as well as in those countries formally allied to the United States.

There can be no question, then, about the importance of the American role in twentieth-century world affairs. But the reasons why America has played this role are not so obvious. Exploring them is not only illuminating in itself but can also help us to understand certain distinctive and persistent features of US foreign policy.

It is clear, of course, that America's influence on world politics has only been made possible by the nation's extraordinary economic pre-eminence. It was in the 1880s that America overtook Britain as the world's leading producer of manufactured goods. For most of the twentieth century, its output of such goods has been more than twice as great as that of any other country; for some years after World War II, it was almost equal to that of the rest of the world combined.[3] This productive capacity, in combination with advanced technology and a large and comparatively well-educated population, has provided the basis not only for formidable military strength but also for the provision of foreign aid (both economic and military), and the development of a large and sophisticated apparatus for the conduct of foreign policy, including the gathering of intelligence.

Command of such resources has been a necessary condition of America's world role. It is seen by some as also a sufficient explanation for it. For the political scientist Robert Gilpin, for example, it is axiomatic that: 'As the power of a state increases, it seeks to extend its territorial control, its political influence, and/or its domination of the international economy. . . . The phenomenon . . . is universal.'[4] As with other supposedly universal patterns, this is often explained in terms of human nature. 'Of the gods we believe and of men we know that it is a necessary law of their nature that they rule wherever they can,' Thucydides has the Athenians telling the Melians. This aphorism is cited by Hans J. Morgenthau in support of his assertion that the drive to dominate is one of 'those elemental biopsychological drives by which in turn society is created'.[5] Such an assumption apparently underlies the common image of power as a sort of liquid substance, flowing automatically into hollows and 'vacuums'.

To other 'realist' writers, however, the imperatives of power derive less from some internally generated drive to dominate than from the demands of the international system. Kenneth Waltz, for example, has observed that 'in a world of nation-states, some regulation of military, political, and economic affairs is at times badly needed'. On this view, such regulation and the provision of other 'collective goods' inevitably falls upon the shoulders of the larger states since 'great power gives its possessors a big stake in the system and the ability to act for its sake'.[6] The idea that the international system imposes special tasks on its most powerful members has been most developed in the version known as 'the theory of hegemonic stability'. According to this theory, a multilateral trading system can only function successfully when there is a 'hegemon' to manage it, ensure an acceptable distribution of benefits, and when necessary enforce adherence to the rules. In the nineteenth century and until 1914, it is said, this role was played by Britain; since World War II it has been assumed by the USA. 'A liberal economic system is not self-sustaining,' Robert Gilpin has insisted, 'but is maintained only through the actions – initiatives, bargaining, and sanctions – of the dominant power.'[7]

Whether they focus on internal or external dynamics, theories that assume that the possession of power will automatically lead to its exercise are open to the objection that they neglect the costs of wielding power. For, of course, every means by which a state can exert leverage in international affairs involves some sacrifice on its part. This is obvious in the case of wars, where the price takes the form of casualties as well as money. But it also applies to the deployment (or even maintenance in being) of armed forces, military or other foreign aid, economic sanctions or preferential terms for trade or investment. These last, as Klaus Knorr has pointed out, always involve some sort of opportunity cost through 'diverting trade or capital investments from the channels indicated by purely economic criteria'.[8] Recognizing that the exercise of power requires effortful activity involving the sacrifice of other desirable goods makes it much less plausible to see it simply as a universal human instinct. The psychological restraints on the drive to domination do not consist only of altruistic feelings and ethical considerations; they may also include the desire for an easy and comfortable life. These restraints are only likely to be overcome if the benefits to be gained appear to outweigh the costs.

That these are not merely theoretical objections is well illustrated by the case of the United States itself. As we have seen, its latent power has been greater than that of any other state throughout the century. In terms of steelmaking capacity, for example – which Winston Churchill described as 'a rather decisive index of conventional military power' – the United States in 1913 possessed about twice that of Germany, which in turn produced more steel than Britain, France and Russia combined.[9] In 1920, after the European powers had suffered the devastating effects of World War I, the United States produced 59 per cent of the world's steel – a proportion even higher than in the years following World War II.[10] Yet in the 1920s and 1930s the United States did not deploy any significant portion of the country's ample resources in efforts to affect the course of events in the outside world. Its definition of its security interests did not expand beyond the western hemisphere and it did not assume any responsibility for managing either the international economic system or the world balance of power.

When we ask why this was so, we can find reasons both in the internal character of the United States – its political system and the nature of its society – and in certain objective aspects of its relationship to the rest of the world. The United States is not only a democracy but it is one in which the legislative branch is much less amenable to executive leadership than in most other democracies. In 1919–20, it was the Senate that prevented the United States from taking part in Wilson's League of Nations, and Congress remained an important constraint on American foreign policy throughout the interwar period – keeping the nation out of the World Court as well as the League of Nations, ruling out any forgiving of the war debts, and passing the neutrality legislation of 1935–7. But the attitudes of the Congress reflected the introversion of most Americans, whose attention (and that of their media) was almost wholly devoted to the excitements and problems of their enormous country. (Even in the 1970s, only about 6 per cent of Americans held passports.)[11]

On the other hand, there is nothing peculiarly American about the reluctance of ordinary people to bear the costs of a strenuous foreign policy – whether these come in the form of casualties, conscription, taxes, or other forms of inconvenience. There always has to be some countervailing benefit to provide an incentive. The difficulty for those Americans who wanted their country to play a much more active role in world affairs – and there were always such people, from the days of Theodore Roosevelt at the beginning of the century – was to make a convincing case that the United States had enough to stake to justify the sacrifices that would inevitably be involved in the exercise of power abroad. The most universal and generally the most important of such stakes are economic well-being and security from attack. But in the case of the United States it was hard to show that either of these bedrock national interests depended upon the achievement of any particular foreign policy goals.

As far as the nation's prosperity was concerned, this seemed to be overwhelmingly dependent on developments at home. In the 1920s, only about 5 per cent of America's GNP was exported and in the 1930s less than 4 per cent. (These percentages, low as they are in comparative terms, would be reduced even further if the North American economy were considered as a unit, since between a fifth and a quarter of US exports have been to Canada and Mexico.)[12] The proportion of American capital invested abroad was even lower –

about 3 per cent.[13] Imports ran at a slightly lower level than exports and included only a few raw materials not available within the nation's borders. (In this period the United States itself was by far the world's biggest oil producer.) Moreover, such overseas economic interests as America had – in the form of markets, investments or sources of vital imports – made few demands on US foreign policy. For one thing, the sheer size of the American economy meant that America's trade relations were in every case proportionately more important to the other country involved than they were to the United States itself.

The United States seemed at least equally self-sufficient in terms of security. It is true that from the early twentieth century it was argued by some of those who wanted America to become more actively involved in international politics that the protection provided by the great oceans in the nineteenth century had been undermined by modern technology. This was said first of the steamship, and later of the development of aviation. But these arguments were weak. The transition from sail to steam, for example, reduced the range of battleships and thus made the oceans more, not less, of a barrier to hostile navies. As John Keegan has delighted in pointing out, the 'wooden walls' of Nelson's day had a range far greater than that of later 'fossil-fuel fleets', constrained 'by the capacity of their coal bunkers or oil tankers'.[14] Likewise, the dependence of modern armies on sophisticated and customized munitions meant that a trans-oceanic invasion would face much greater logistical problems than had been the case during the War of 1812 (when the British had burnt down Washington). And with the development of aviation, any invading force would also need to achieve air supremacy over the North American coastline – in the face of a defending airforce that would be infinitely nearer to its bases. Given America's productive capacity it was almost inconceivable that this could be achieved, and so it is not surprising that most Americans, including the nation's military leaders, had implicit faith in their country's ability to defend itself without the help of allies.

So there seems no necessary or inevitable reason why the United States should not have continued along the path it followed in the 1920s and 1930s – even though this involved punching much less than its potential weight in world politics. To establish why it did not, it is clear that we have to look at the 1940s. The ten years that separated the fall of France from the outbreak of the Korean War witnessed a revolution in American foreign policy.[15] At the beginning of 1940, the United States was still following a policy of unilateral non-involvement; by the end of 1950, it had not only assumed the leadership of such international organizations as the UN, the IMF, the World Bank and GATT, but also committed substantial resources to efforts to affect the course of political developments across the globe.

Many historians (and even more political scientists) have a simple explanation for this dramatic change – which is that now (at last) a vital national interest was clearly at stake: the danger that the whole of Eurasia would fall under the domination of a hostile regime – first Hitler and then the Kremlin – posed a threat to America's own security that *had* to be resisted. However, this seems to me a seriously misleading interpretation of history. In the first place, it is by no means self-evident that the security of North America *was* in real danger – or that most Americans ever thought it was. The arguments about the enormous technical difficulties that would confront a transoceanic assault remained valid – and were thoroughly rehearsed by isolationist spokesmen such as Charles Lindbergh in the fierce debates of 1940–1 over the course the United States should follow. That most Americans (including, incidentally, the military leadership) remained convinced that the United States could, if necessary, defend itself unaided seems to be shown by the fact that they did not favour actual participation in World War II until Pearl Harbor, even though there had been a good chance that the war would end in an early victory for the Axis ever since the fall of France in the summer of 1940.

A second reason why we need to seek for a more complicated explanation of America's assumption of a leading role in world politics is that the nature of the foreign policy-making process in the United States makes single-cause explanations inherently improbable. It may be possible to understand British policy in the nineteenth century by studying 'the official mind', but certainly in the American case we need to concern ourselves with more than the minds of a small number of officials. Any policy that makes a significant demand upon resources has to have a broad and deep basis of political support if it is to be sustained. Although policy-makers, and particularly the president, have several important assets in developing such public support, they cannot, in an open and competitive political system, take it for granted. Developing the necessary consensus behind a foreign policy of any significant degree of strenuousness is a process very similar to that required to put into effect a domestic policy. Generally, it, too, involves mustering a congressional majority – whether for a declaration of war or a treaty or, more commonly, for the appropriation of the necessary funds. Such a process requires an aggregation of support, which is almost always the product of a coming together of people and groups with various interests and priorities, and also of individuals who are themselves responsive to more than one type of appeal.

Once we look at things this way, we see that support for the policy of aiding the Allies – the policy that eventually led to Pearl Harbor and American participation in the war – was composed of many elements, several of which ante-dated the 1940s. There is firstly that fact that many Americans, especially in elite circles on the eastern seaboard, had long felt that the United States should employ more of its potential power in efforts to promote international peace and stability – the Council on Foreign Relations in New York propagated the views of such people. From late 1938, President Franklin Roosevelt and leading members of his administration had wished to throw at least some of America's power into the scales against Hitler. Jewish-Americans and Americans who identified closely with Britain were, for obvious reasons, among those who were particularly keen for action of this kind.

More broadly, three more general factors can be identified. The first is commonly overlooked, particularly by political scientists seeking to account for American 'globalism' in terms of mechanistic models of international relations. It is the sense of involvement with Europe, the continent from which had come the families of the great majority of Americans (and of nearly all those who voted) and with which the United States shared a civilization. To gauge the significance of this, let us imagine that the economic and strategic relationship between the United States and Europe had been exactly as it was but that Europe had been inhabited by peoples with whom Americans had little cultural connection, such as Hindus or Muslims. Would the 'objective' imperatives of national interest have still led to the same degree of political involvement and military commitment?

Secondly, there was the deep-rooted sense that the United States bore a special responsibility for the survival and the success in the world of liberty and democracy. Lacking an ethnic basis, American nationalism has always been essentially ideological in character, and from the beginning its values have been seen as universal ones. The idea that it was America's mission to demonstrate to the world the viability of a free society and democratic government had been a staple of Fourth of July orations long before Lincoln invoked it in his Gettysburg Address. For Lincoln as for most nineteenth-century Americans, the nation's role was simply to provide an example to the world, and the more evangelical interpretation of this sense of mission was only really developed by Woodrow Wilson in justifying intervention in World War I. The disappointments of that crusade had led to a general feeling that the sacrifices involved had been greater than the benefits and that the nation should stick to its traditional, purely exemplary, role. But Wilson's activist interpretation of the nation's mission was reinvigorated by the prospect of a Nazi-dominated world. 'America does not belong entirely to us,' Henry Luce told his countrymen as France was falling. 'A little of America belongs to every man and woman everywhere who has had faith in democracy and hope in a world of peace and justice . . . . We the living who control the destiny of America today are the heirs of a great inheritance from men who lived and from men who died to make men free.'[16]

Thirdly, and crucially, there was a sense of America's great power. This seems to have operated in at least two ways. In the first place, it induced confidence that America *could* make a difference – indeed, quite possibly at relatively low cost to itself. We have become used to the remarkably low casualties suffered by the United States in its recent technologically sophisticated military actions, but even in 1940–1 it seems that most Americans hoped that America's economic power would be enough to contain Hitler and Japan without the need for full-scale belligerency. But the second way in which the confidence in American power seems to have prompted action is by generating a sense of responsibility. Again, no one expressed this better than Luce, whose essay on 'The American Century' was written as a contribution to the debate over Lend-Lease. Noting that 'almost every expert will agree that Britain cannot win complete victory – cannot even, in the common saying, "stop Hitler" – without American help', he called on his countrymen 'to accept wholeheartedly our duty and our opportunity as the most powerful and vital nation in the world, and in consequence to exert upon the world the full impact of our influence': 'America is responsible, to herself as well as to history, for the world-environment in which she lives.'[17]

World War II brought many more Americans to this way of thinking. After the event, American involvement was taken to have shown the unrealism of isolationism and there was general support in 1944–5 for America's leading role in establishing the United Nations and 'the Bretton Woods system', including the IMF and World Bank. However, peace still brought a cry to 'bring the boys home', and a consequent precipitous decline in the strength of America's armed forces from over 12 million in June 1945 to one and a half million two years later.[18] It was only the Cold War that induced Congress to reverse the trend and to undertake the extensive foreign policy commitments that it did in the late 1940s and subsequently.

The combination of impulses and constituencies that sustained the Cold War was larger and more various than that which had supported the policy of aid to the Allies before World War II. The long-standing internationalists and anti-Fascist liberals of 1940–1 were now joined by formerly isolationist conservatives and anti-British ethnic groups. Almost everyone could sign on for a confrontation with Soviet Russia since Communism was seen as the enemy of all that most Americans believed in – not only the free enterprise system but also religion. Denunciations of it, particularly by Catholic spokesmen, had hardly been abated by the wartime alliance with Russia; FDR had felt the need to emphasize that 'the Nazis are as ruthless as the Communists in their denial of God'.[19]

The missing element remained any persuasive connection between America's foreign policy and the country's core material interests. This may seem surprising in light of the fact that with the development of intercontinental bombers and missiles, together with nuclear weapons, a devastating attack upon the American homeland did become technically feasible in a way that it had never been before. Since then ('Star Wars' notwithstanding), it has been deterrence rather than defence upon which the United States has relied for protection. But deterrence rests on the nation's retaliatory (second-strike) capability and this has been entirely self-generated. Indeed, a good case can be made that the physical security of the United States in the nuclear age has been reduced rather than increased by its involvement in world politics, and especially by its commitment to 'extended deterrence' (that is, the threat to engage in nuclear war for the protection of other countries). As was observed many years ago by that tough-minded political scientist Robert W. Tucker, 'the loss of allies, even the most important allies, would not significantly alter the prospects of an adversary surviving an attack upon the United States' but 'the risks that might have to be run on behalf of allies could lead to a nuclear confrontation that would escape the control of the great protagonists'.[20]

Nor did America's economic interests provide much of a justification for an extensive foreign policy. The nation's prosperity continued to depend, almost as largely as it had in the interwar period, on its domestic production and market – exports remaining at little more than 4 per cent of GNP. It is true that the proportion of capital exported grew more but this, too, remained low in comparative terms. Even in 1968, following two decades in which more capital flowed out of the United States than at any time before or since, direct investment abroad represented only about 6 per cent of total American investment, and the return on foreign investment amounted to only 9.3 per cent of domestic corporate profits. (And again, the proportion invested in Canada was approximately equal to that invested in the whole of Europe.)[21] More significant, without doubt, was America's increased dependence on imports of oil, which by the 1980s amounted to about a third of the country's enormous consumption. These imports, despite being much smaller proportionately than those of Japan and many Western European countries, were clearly vital in maintaining the American standard of living but it was less clear that they were dependent on US diplomatic or military commitments; the oil producers needed buyers and there was no substitute for the American market.

The point here is not to deny that the need to protect American security or American prosperity has been urged as the reason for overseas commitments – clearly it often has been. But the underlying realities have been such that this argument could always be persuasively questioned, and this has reduced the extent to which they have been able, by themselves, to sustain foreign policy enterprises that made large demands upon American resources.

This may, indeed, be seen as another – rarely remarked – aspect of American exceptionalism. As a state in a world of states, the USA in the twentieth century has been in an unparalleled position, not only because of the sheer scale of its power but also because of the almost negligible demands that have been made upon that power by the core national interests of economic well-being and physical security. It has *had* to do very little, but it has had the capacity to do a great deal. In other words, the United States as a nation–state has possessed a uniquely wide range of choice between viable options in the field of foreign policy.

Adopting this perspective helps us to understand several persistent characteristics of US foreign policy. One is the amount of internal argument there has been about it – for when there is a choice between viable options, disagreement is likely to arise. The history of US foreign policy in the twentieth century is punctuated by 'Great Debates' – over imperialism following the War of 1898, over intervention in World War I, over the League of Nations, over aid to the Allies in 1940–1, over the re-commitment of troops to Europe in 1950, over Vietnam. Even the Persian Gulf War against Iraq, it is now generally forgotten, was opposed by many before it began, and the resolution giving the president authority to use force to end the illegal occupation of Kuwait passed the Senate by a margin of only five votes.[22]

Secondly, and relatedly, this perspective helps to explain the oscillations that have occurred – the imperialist episode at the turn of the century and the reaction against it, intervention in World War I and the interwar reaction against that, the rejection of the League of Nations in 1920 and the formation of the UN in 1945, involvement in Vietnam and the reaction against that.

These oscillations are themselves only the most dramatic instances of a general tendency towards what might be called unsteadiness or lack of resolve in pursuit of foreign policy objectives. Many observers have commented on the gap that has frequently opened up between the declared aims of American policy and the making of a serious effort to achieve them – preserving an 'Open Door' in China being a much-cited example in this regard. Such frailty is easier to understand if one recognizes that the United States pays a small price for foreign policy failures. After all, what apart from some prestige and self-esteem, did the United States lose by losing in Vietnam? If one wants to see how foreign policy gains both focus and force when there is a lot at stake, consider the contrasting case of Israel.

Mention of Israel reminds us that the sense that the United States has had, as it were, power 'surplus to requirements' has led other countries (not least Britain) to look to it for help. Such countries have been able to take advantage of the American political system to gain degrees of leverage that would have been difficult in a more centralized and bureaucratic decision-making process. But the same sense of a margin of safety may also have encouraged American leaders to use foreign policy as an instrument in domestic politics, by catering to the interests or prejudices of groups with electoral clout. At its extreme this can give the impression that the outside world is being treated as no more than a backdrop, against which Americans are working out their domestic conflicts and psycho-dramas.

This image is a caricature, of course, and does no sort of justice to the depth of knowledge, intelligence and sense of involvement that a significant minority of Americans bring to foreign affairs. Nonetheless, it would be true to say that non-Americans visiting the United States are frequently struck by how unimportant – if not unreal – the outside world seems to be to most Americans. Such introversion has seemed to many both surprising and inappropriate for the inhabitants of a country whose influence beyond its borders has been so enormous for so long. But this disjunction becomes more understandable if we attribute it, not to the peculiarly benighted character of Americans, but to their remarkably fortunate situation. With neither their security nor their great prosperity depending much upon events overseas, they have had less incentive than most to learn about foreign countries, and more generally it is this disjunction between power and need which helps to account for the vagaries of US foreign policy during the American century.

Notes and References

Parts of this essay previously appeared in Alex Danchev (ed.), *Fin de Siècle: The Meaning of the Twentieth Century* (London, 1995), and are re-published here with the kind permission of Alex Danchev.

1 'The American Century', *Life*, 10/7 (17 Feb. 1941), pp. 61–5 at 64.

2 Paul Kennedy, *The Rise and Fall of the Great Powers: Economic Change and Military Conflict from 1500 to 2000* (London, 1988), pp. 353–6.

3 Paul Bairoch, 'International Industrialization Levels from 1750 to 1980', *Journal of European Economic History*, 11 (Fall, 1982), pp. 296, 304.

4 Robert Gilpin, *War and Change in World Politics* (Cambridge, 1981), pp. 106–7.

5 Morgenthau seems to have seen this as one of the 'objective laws that have their roots in human nature' upon which he sought to erect his 'theory of international politics'. Hans J. Morgenthau, *Politics Among Nations*, 3rd edn (New York, 1965), pp. 33–5, 3–4. Thucydides's sentence has been frequently quoted. Colin S. Gray is a recent writer for whom it captures 'the permanent realities of international politics'. *The Geopolitics of Super Power* (Lexington, Ky, 1988), p. 33.

6 Kenneth N. Waltz, *Theory of International Politics* (Reading, MA, 1979), pp. 195–209. Quotations on pp. 207, 195.

7 Robert Gilpin, *US Power and the Multinational Corporation: The Political Economy of Foreign Direct Investment* (London, 1976), p. 85.

8 Klaus Knorr, *The Power of Nations: The Political Economy of International Relations* (New York, 1975), p. 94.

9 Kennedy, *The Rise and Fall of the Great Powers*, p. 200. For the Churchill quotation, see Peter G. Boyle (ed.), *The Churchill–Eisenhower Correspondence, 1953–1955* (Chapel Hill and London, 1990), p. 179.

10 Duncan Burn, *The Steel Industry 1939–1959: A Study in Competition and Planning* (Cambridge, 1961), table 105.

11 At a time when passports were valid for five years, 13,907,633 passports were issued in the five years 1974–8 inclusive. The population of the USA was 203,212,000 in 1970 and 226,546,000 in 1980. Information from State Department website. http://www.travel.state.gov/passport; B.R. Mitchell, *International Historical Statistics: The Americas, 1750–1993*, 4th edn (London and New York, 1998), p. 6.

12 US Bureau of the Census, *Historical Statistics of the United States: Colonial Times to 1970* (Washington, DC, 1975), pp. 887, 903.

13 Waltz, *Theory of International Politics*, p. 213.

14 John Keegan, *The Price of Admiralty: The Evolution of Naval Warfare* (Harmondsworth, Middlesex, 1988), pp. 41–2.
15 William G. Carleton, *The Revolution in American Foreign Policy: Its Global Range* (New York, 1963).
16 'America and Armageddon', *Life*, 8/23 (3 June 1940), pp. 40, 100. This article was the text of a speech delivered by Luce over the NBC network on 22 May 1940.
17 'The American Century', pp. 62–3.
18 Robert A. Pollard, *Economic Security and the Origins of the Cold War, 1945–1950* (New York, 1985), p. 22.
19 Radio Address, 27 May 1941. *The Public Papers and Addresses of Franklin D. Roosevelt 1941* (New York, 1950), pp. 181–94 at 184.
20 Robert W. Tucker, *A New Isolationism: Threat or Promise?* (New York, 1972), pp. 46–7; *The Purposes of American Power: An Essay on National Security* (New York, 1981), p. 121; 'Containment and the Search for Alternatives: A Critique', in Aaron Wildavsky (ed.), *Beyond Containment: Alternative American Policies toward the Soviet Union* (San Francisco, 1983), pp. 81–2.
21 Robert W. Tucker, *The Radical Left and American Foreign Policy* (Baltimore, MD, and London, 1971), pp. 128–9.
22 The Senate vote was 52 to 47. The House of Representatives approved the resolution by 250 votes to 183. *New York Times*, 13 January 1991.

QUENTIN SKINNER

Visions of Civil Liberty

Politicians like to reassure us that they feel a special tenderness towards the ideal of liberty, while political philosophers generally agree that the preservation of civil liberty is one of the principal duties of the state. But what exactly are these distinguished figures talking about when they hold forth to us in this way about the value of our freedom and the need to sustain it?

When we listen to politicians, it is often painfully evident that they have no very clear idea of what they are talking about at all. But among professional political philosophers – at least among the best of them – it is usually clear enough, so let me begin with them. More specifically, let me begin with John Rawls, perhaps the most influential political philosopher of the present generation, at least within the Anglophone tradition, and to the account of liberty he offers in his treatise *A Theory of Justice*, originally published in 1971. Rawls argues that all our talk about liberty (or, at least, all our coherent talk) points to a concept with a triadic character.[1] Of the three elements in the triad, the first is obviously that we must have in mind some agent or agency, some person or institution, that can be said to possess, or not possess, freedom of action. Next, we must be talking about the powers or abilities of such agents, about the range of actions they are capable of performing at will. Finally, if we are to say of such agents that they are free to act or forbear from acting at will, what will have to be shown is that they are unconstrained by any coercive influences from the exercise of their abilities or powers.

The concept of liberty is thus taken to be a 'negative' one. According to this analysis, the presence of liberty is always marked by the absence of something, and specifically by the absence of some external interference that serves to limit the capacity of an agent to pursue his or her chosen ends. These coercive influences, it is assumed, can in turn operate either on the body or on the will. If you are physically prevented from acting (or physically forced to act) then you are unfree: unfree to act in the first instance, unfree not to act in the second. But equally, if you are threatened with dire consequence should you choose to act (or fail to act) in some particular way, such that your will is coerced, then you are again unfree: unfree to act except as coercively demanded. Summarizing, we can say that on this account the idea of liberty is simply that of being unconstrained by external interference from the exercise of your powers.

Nowadays this is by far the most widespread way of thinking about human freedom. But if we are historians we shall want to know more than this; we shall want to know what happens if we move back in time and ask how the concept was understood and employed in earlier periods. Suppose we move back as much as a hundred years. Perhaps the greatest work of Anglophone political philosophy written at the end of the nineteenth century – a work in many ways comparable with Rawls's at the end of the twentieth – was Henry Sidgwick's *The Elements of Politics*, which first appeared in 1891. What does Sidgwick have to tell us about the meaning or definition of liberty? He maintains that the term 'signifies primarily the absence of physical coercion or confinement', but adds that 'in another part of its meaning' it is 'opposed not to physical constraint, but to the moral constraint placed on inclination by the fear of painful consequences'.[2] What we learn from Sidgwick, in short, is no different from what we learned from Rawls. Both assume that the presence of freedom is signified by the absence of some external constraint upon the will or body of an agent that prevents them from acting as they desire.

What if we now go back in time as much as another hundred years? Within the Anglophone tradition, the most widely read treatise on the theory of politics at the end of the eighteenth century was undoubtedly William Paley's *The Principles of Moral and Political Philosophy*, first published in 1785. What do we learn from the section in which Paley offers to define for us the concept of civil liberty? We learn that, as he declares, 'the degree of actual liberty' always bears 'a reversed proportion to the number and severity of the restrictions' placed upon it.[3] We learn, in short, that freedom consists in the absence of such restrictions or constraints. But this, again, is no different from what we have already learned from Sidgwick and, more recently, from Rawls.

We may well feel inclined to stop at this point. After all, how much history do we need? Having encountered so much consensus over such a long period, it may seem natural to conclude that we have uncovered not merely 'our' way of thinking about liberty but a sense of how we *need* to think about the concept if we are to speak coherently. But no such inference will strike an historian as at all sensible. To gain as full as possible an understanding of our fundamental concepts, we need to be ready to survey not merely the recent past, nor even the past millennium, but the entire history of our culture. We need to be prepared, in other words, to begin at the beginning, which in the case of moral and political philosophy means beginning with classical Greece and Rome.

One of the founding texts for the study of freedom in civil associations is Plato's *Republic*, in Book IV of which the figure of Socrates raises the question of what it means to act freely.[4] His account initially looks familiar, for he agrees that it involves the exercise of our powers at will. But his ensuing argument is not familiar at all, for he adds that our active spirit can attach itself either to our reason or to our appetites, and that whenever we allow ourselves to act in line with our mere appetites we enslave ourselves. So freedom is not a matter of being unconstrained from exercising our powers, since no one who exercises their powers uncontrolled by reason can be said to act freely. We act freely only if we choose rationally.

Suppose we shift our attention from ancient Greece to ancient Rome. Do we begin to encounter a more recognizable understanding of civil liberty at that stage in our history? It might appear that we do, for the claim that law exists to uphold the freedom of citizens is emphatically stated at the outset of the *Digest* of Roman Law. Moreover, the definition of civil liberty offered in the *Digest* appears at first sight a conventional one, based as it is on equating the freedom of citizens with the condition of being *sui iuris*, capable of acting according to their own wills and in their own right.[5]

If we ask, however, about the circumstances in which we may be said to forfeit this freedom, the answer we are given begins to look rather less recognizable. We lose our liberty, according to the *Digest*, when we suffer enslavement, and the condition of slavery is defined not as a state in which we are constrained from acting at will, but rather as a condition of dependence in which we are subject to the will – and hence to the arbitrary domination – of someone else. The condition of freedom is accordingly envisaged not as a state in which we are unconstrained from exercising our powers at will, but rather as a state in which we are secured from the danger of being subjected to arbitrary constraint. We may remain unfree, on this analysis, even if we are never threatened or coerced. For we may live in conditions of dependence on the goodwill of others, and to live in such conditions is to be deprived of our liberty.

This contrast between freedom and servitude, and its attendant analysis of unfreedom in terms of dependence, was to remain the orthodox way of thinking about the concept of civil liberty for at least a millennium. The same analysis underlies the distinction between villeins and free subjects in medieval law, and surfaces again in the attempts of the city-republics of early Renaissance Italy to vindicate their independence from the Holy Roman Empire. Finally, the same view of what it means to live 'in a free state' provides the animating principle of the great republican treatises of the high Renaissance, culminating in Machiavelli's *Discourses* of 1519 on Livy's history of Rome. For these writers, the contrast in the case of political as well as individual human bodies is always between living in freedom and living in conditions of domination and servitude.

I began with the modern idea that freedom consists in the absence of external constraint. While this is often taken to be the only coherent way of thinking about the concept, it now appears that the concept was hardly ever analysed in this way until some time after the era of the Renaissance. I hope that this example, sketchy though it has been, may perhaps do something to suggest why our historical perspectives need to encompass millennia rather than merely the recent centuries on which so many historians are content to concentrate. One value of such long-range studies is that they help to liberate us from the parochialism of our own forms of cultural analysis and criticism, and to open up alternative ways of thinking about some of our deepest commitments. But a further value is that they enable us to start asking historical questions about ourselves. Two such questions immediately spring to mind in the light of what I have said about the history of our thinking about civil liberty. When did we first start to suppose that the right way to analyse the concept is simply in terms of absence of constraint? And what has led so many writers to insist that this highly simplified analysis is the only coherent one that can be given?

As far as I can see, the earliest writer in the Anglophone tradition to present a systematic account of the modern theory was Thomas Hobbes in his *Leviathan* of 1651. Nowadays Hobbes's analysis is liable to look somewhat obvious, but as soon as we reflect on what had gone before we can see that it constituted, in its time, an astonishingly bold assault on the whole tradition of classical thought.

Hobbes is one of the leading systematic philosophers of the scientific revolution, and is typical of his age in aspiring to reduce the complexity of appearances to some simple and basic categories. The fundamental claim to which this ambition led him was that the entire world – however it may appear to us – is in truth nothing other than matter in motion. It follows that even such a seemingly inescapable moral concept as freedom makes sense only if it can be applied, as Hobbes puts it, 'no less to Irrational and Inanimate creatures, than to rational'.[6] To take Hobbes's own example in *Leviathan*, what we say about freedom must be capable of applying equally to human bodies and to such cases as bodies of water. To say of a body of water that it is free is merely to say that it is externally unobstructed from moving according to its nature. So too with the freedom of human bodies, which for Hobbes amounts to nothing more than the absence of external impediments upon their capacity to exercise their powers.

Hobbes's account of freedom is recognizably the modern one with which I began, and he presents it in an especially stringent form. Freedom, for Hobbes, is absence of external constraint and nothing more. Free action for Hobbes is merely unimpeded action; it is never freely willed action. This is because, in a universe consisting of nothing more than matter in motion, there is no place for the idea of the freedom of the will. To believe that you possess it is an illusion. When you move freely, this is not because you freely will to move and then move; it is simply because your movement is unconstrained.

We can now see that what Paley, Sidgwick and their successors have done is simply to adopt and inflect this Hobbesian vision of liberty. While they have succeeded in turning it into an orthodoxy, however, they have done so only at the cost of devaluing or dismissing many other traditions of thinking about the subject. I want to end by considering two such traditions, both of which offer a powerful and thought-provoking challenge to prevailing orthodoxies.

Suppose we concede that liberty is best understood as absence of constraint. We can still ask – this is the first challenge I want to consider – what grounds we have for supposing that liberty can be undermined only by external forms of constraint. What about the possibility that the agent undermining your liberty might be you yourself? To raise this question is recognizably to revert to Plato's suggestion that, if I act out of appetite and not out of reason, I constrain myself from acting freely, a suggestion which has been developed in two distinct strands of modern social thought.

One has centred on the idea of inauthenticity. John Stuart Mill offers a celebrated version of the argument in Chapter 3 of his essay *On Liberty* of 1859. I may be so cowed by the conventions of my society that I accept and internalize them until they become second nature. I will no longer feel unfree, even though I may have closed off many options of self-development, for it will no longer occur to me, as Mill puts it, 'to have any inclination except for what is customary', so that I will exercise my choices 'only among things commonly done'.[7] But as Mill goes on to emphasize, what I am doing is constraining myself from fulfilling my own potentialities. This is obviously not an external form of constraint, but it is nevertheless a limitation on my liberty. Fascinatingly, Mill's argument comes remarkably close to the theory of false consciousness that Karl Marx was to articulate so soon afterwards.

The other major thinker who further developed the insight that we may be capable of undermining our own freedom was Sigmund Freud. As Freud himself suggests, psychoanalysis can be construed as a technique for liberating ourselves from self-enslavement. The key concept here is the unconscious, which for Freud contains motives and hence gives rise to actions. But the motives we repress into the unconscious, so that we have no direct access to them, are prone to give rise to neurotic and obsessional forms of behaviour. The psychoanalytic therapy that Freud joined to his explanatory theory was conceived as a means of putting us back in touch with our repressed motivations, thereby liberating ourselves from the obsessional forms of action to which they characteristically give rise. The aspiration, as Freud expressed it, was to make the ego master once more in its own house. Again, the way in which this greater freedom is said to be achieved is by removing constraints on our behaviour placed in our pathway by ourselves.

The other challenge to the mainstream understanding of freedom is a yet more radical one. I want to end by considering two important strands of thought in which the idea of liberty as absence of constraint is wholly repudiated. One involves a restatement of the Roman assumption that freedom resides in the absence of dependence rather than constraint, and hence requires that we be protected from the possibility of being arbitrarily constrained. We find this analysis revived and developed by the enemies of Hobbes in the course of the English constitutional upheavals of the seventeenth century, and above all by James Harrington in his *Oceana* of 1656. Later we find a similar theory articulated by the proponents of republicanism in the French Enlightenment, especially by Jean-Jacques Rousseau in his *Social Contract* of 1762. In our own time a comparable analysis has been further developed by a number of political philosophers – most notably Philip Pettit – in such a way as to offer a direct challenge to conventional liberal pieties.[8]

The anxiety common to these republican writers arises from the condition they describe as executive tyranny, the holding by governments of discretionary powers outside the law. The very presence of such powers, they contend, is enough to undermine our civil liberty, since the knowledge that our rulers possess such powers will be sufficient to inhibit us from challenging them. This is why, according to these theorists, it is indispensable to the preservation of civil liberty that all legal systems should include a bill of rights placing our fundamental liberties beyond the reach of executive powers. The claim is not that, in the absence of such guarantees, our civil liberty will be less secure; it is rather that it will already be forfeited, since we shall be condemned to living in dependence on the goodwill of our government.

I turn finally from the heritage of Rome to that of Greece, and thus to the other school of thought in which the idea of liberty as absence of constraint has continued to be repudiated. The argument in this case is again rooted in the Platonic suggestion that rational action is alone free. To advance this claim is obviously to reject the view that we are free so long as we are able to act at will; it is to claim instead that the question of whether we are acting freely depends on what exactly is willed. The idea of freedom, in the fully developed form of this theory, thus comes to be seen not as absence of constraint on action but rather as action of a certain kind. But action of what kind? Of such a kind, it is suggested, as will enable us most fully to realize our nature and its potentialities. So our freedom, on this analysis, becomes the name of our highest moral achievement, the name of that state in which we shall have attained what we have it in us to become.

This theory only makes sense on the assumption that we have distinctive goals as human beings, and that we are fully or truly free only in the pursuit of them. But there are two deeply influential traditions of thinking about liberty in our culture that have in fact been based on precisely this belief. One is Christian, and assumes that we most fully realize our natures in the service of God. This means that, for a true believer, God's service – in Thomas Cranmer's phrase – will itself be perfect freedom. The other and analogous strand of thinking is Hegelian, and stems from the assumption that our natures are inherently social or political – that man is the political animal, in Aristotle's phrase. For Hegel this in turn means that we are capable of realizing our freedom only as citizens of a modern state. Both these visions assume, as Charles Taylor has recently observed, that freedom is not simply an opportunity concept; it is an exercise concept.[9] To be free, in other words, is not simply a matter of having opportunities for action; it is a matter of exercising those opportunities in a certain way, and specifically in such a way as to realize our human potentialities as fully as possible.

My story has been a somewhat postmodern one, in that it has moved in a circle rather than a line. But even a postmodern story ought perhaps to have a moral, so let me end by drawing what I take to be the moral of this particular tale. The moral is: never ask for *the* analysis of a concept such as civil liberty. To put the point another way: all political theories are prone to degenerate into ideologies. They may be able to offer us perfectly coherent accounts of the key concepts we use to organize our moral and political lives, as the current liberal understanding of the concept of liberty undoubtedly does. But they go too far if they suggest – as many liberal theorists currently do – that their analysis can in turn be used to stigmatize other and rival understandings of the same concept as necessarily confused. To prevent our philosophical reflections from merely serving the times, we need to liberate ourselves from this very natural tendency. We need to recognize that our concepts offer us one way of negotiating the world, but that there may be other and no less coherent readings to be given of them.

How can this kind of liberation be achieved? One way, I have suggested – and perhaps the most illuminating and helpful way – is by studying history. But how much history do we need? As much, I have tried to suggest, as possible. We need to be prepared to encompass not merely the past millennium but earlier millennia too.

Notes and References

1 John Rawls, *A Theory of Justice* (Cambridge, Mass., 1971), p. 202.
2 Henry Sidgwick, *The Elements of Politics* (London, 1891), p. 45.
3 William Paley, 'Of Civil Liberty', in *The Principles of Moral and Political Philosophy* (London, 1785), p. 443.
4 Plato, *The Republic*, ed. G.R.F. Ferrari, trans. Tom Griffith (Cambridge, 2000), Bk IV, esp. pp. 131–41 (and cf. Bk IX, esp. pp. 292–3, 310–11).
5 *Digest* I. 6. 1.
6 Thomas Hobbes, *Leviathan*, ed. Richard Tuck (Cambridge, 1996), p. 145.
7 John Stuart Mill, *On Liberty and Other Writings*, ed. Stefan Collini (Cambridge, 1989), pp. 61–2.
8 See Philip Pettit, *Republicanism: A Theory of Freedom and Government* (Oxford, 1997). I have tried to develop a comparable argument myself: see Quentin Skinner, *Liberty Before Liberalism* (Cambridge, 1998).
9 Charles Taylor, 'What's Wrong with Negative Liberty', in *The Idea of Freedom*, ed. Alan Ryan (Oxford, 1979), p. 177.

PETER CLARKE

The Century of the Hedgehog: The Demise of Political Ideologies in the Twentieth Century

The word 'ideology' came into the English language as an adaptation of the French *idéologie* in 1796 – so the *Oxford English Dictionary* tells us – and it was clearly no coincidence that this happened during the course of the French Revolution, which injected a new dimension into political change that we immediately recognize as ideological. At this time 'ideology' applied to 'the science of ideas; the study and origin of the nature of ideas'. It would thus cover much of what we do in Cambridge under the rubric of the history of ideas. It soon took on an extended second sense applying to 'ideal or abstract speculation or visionary theorizing', for which I shall suggest 'doctrine' is a more helpful term. It is with the *OED*'s third sense that I think we come to the prevailing modern meaning, indicating a system of ideas especially concerning aspects of social life; in particular I will emphasize the definition as 'the manner of thinking *characteristic* of a class or individual'.

My general contention is that the twentieth century saw both the ascendancy and the demise of ideologies as big, simplifying ideas. The image that is irresistible here is the one supplied by Isaiah Berlin when he seized on the proverbial statement that the fox knows many things but the hedgehog knows one big thing. In this sense, the twentieth century was the century of the hedgehog, with big ideas seeking to remake the world – and leaving important consequences that were often unintended.

We can see ideology at work, to use Marx's phrase, 'when theory grips the masses', which he saw as happening when ideas came to inspire and direct the actions of social classes. But we need not be quite so specific as that and might simply say that ideology describes how doctrines acquire political purchase in society.

Of course, this process could be observed well before the twentieth century dawned. The French Revolution notoriously proclaimed three abstract principles – *Liberté*, *Egalité*, *Fraternité* – which fuelled its march across Europe, generating a mass appeal and one that proved enduring. Before that, the United States of America had been founded upon a declaration of independence that proclaimed certain sweeping 'truths' – about equality and about the proper ends of human life – to be 'self-evident', which was a way of winning an argument for certain contentious and highly charged values by assuming that the argument had already been won. Even in England, the 'Good Old Cause' nurtured by the Commonwealthmen who regretted the failure of the Cromwellian revolution saw a sort of clash of ideas as well as material forces that can well be called ideological. And this outlook in turn mobilized and enlisted the values of civic republicanism which stretched back through the Italian city states that flourished during the Renaissance into an appeal to the classical tradition, variously reinvented and reappropriated by its heirs.

Yet the twentieth century, I believe, is distinctive in being dominated by a clash of ideologies, especially those that we can usefully, and not too anachronistically, label as Left versus Right. It takes two sides to make a quarrel, which is perhaps why it took until the twentieth century for this conflict to be joined. Until the twentieth century, I would argue, ideology self-evidently comes from the Left. That is, we are considering axiomatically radical *ideas* which disturb traditional conservative *assumptions*. For the strength of the 'Right' (to use this label in a shorthand way) rested on the whole on the strength of a given social structure and on a pattern of deference and hierarchy that went along with it. It thus rested on unquestioned conventions that habituated people to a certain way of life, reinforced very often by organized religion and by that most potent of all conservative historical forces – apathy. And the only hope for the 'Left', in this stylized model, was clearly to stir up trouble, to foment discontent, to agitate, to politicize the masses – to get some *ideas* into their heads in this way.

The struggles for the suffrage in different countries were characteristically struggles of this kind. The hopes of the Left were always invested in the people, or perhaps more specifically in the working class. So democracy was seen as both an end in itself, as a desirable thing to achieve, and also as a means of producing other kinds of beneficial changes within society that would rightly enthrone the people. Democracy was thus both a desirable process and a means of achieving a desirable outcome.

By the end of the First World War, these struggles had been won, in rhetoric if not always in reality. Just as the entry of the USA into the war transformed the struggle on the ground, so it also transformed the rhetoric which justified the struggle. Few on the Allied side, whatever their previous reservations, raised difficulties when President Wilson in 1917 declared the war aim of making the world 'safe for democracy'. These were powerful legitimating pressures, making the idea of universal suffrage unstoppable – even for women, who made notable strides both in Britain and the USA in the aftermath of the war (though it is worth recalling that woman suffrage did not come in France until 1948 and in Switzerland not until the close of the century).

And yet, the twentieth century has not belonged to the Left, least of all in this country. If we look at the experience of democratic politics in the United Kingdom since 1918, which was when the largest step was made towards a universal suffrage, we find that in the eighty years between 1918 and 1997, it wasn't the Left that was running British politics, not for three-quarters of the time: it was the Conservatives and their allies. And much the same pattern would apply in many other comparable Western countries. Nor, despite intermittent talk of the end of ideology, did the centre generally benefit.

What we see, in fact, in the twentieth century is a great clash of ideologies. Marxism was clearly the great model here, but one that was countered and mimicked in significant ways on the Right. Thus Fascism was created fairly self-consciously almost as a mirror image to Marxism. When we talk of Fascism mimicking Marxism, we need go no further than the career of Benito Mussolini to see how this act was performed – Mussolini, whose own political roots, of course, had been on the Left initially.

The novelty of Fascism was to politicize the masses from the right. This is what made Fascism new, and there was therefore an awkward accommodation with the traditional Right, with its historic appeals to legitimacy, resting on largely conventional and historic assumptions. We can see this very clearly in the case of Germany in the early 1930s, when the two great forces on the right, the Nazis with Hitler as their leader, and the Nationalists still looking to Hindenburg, subsisted in a very uneasy relationship.

Fascism – and this applies, of course, to its Nazi variant too – was a radical Right. It had its own populist slogans and beliefs and agenda, stirring up trouble, fomenting discontent, raising the political temperature – just as much as any movement from the Left. It is this, I think, that makes it an ideology and makes it important.

By contrast, Fascist doctrine turned out to be not very interesting. True, some writers who were indiscriminately conscripted and selectively pillaged as precursors of Fascism – Nietzsche, Pareto, Croce, for example – are well worth reading in themselves. Yet there remains little intellectual legacy from explicitly Fascist thinkers in generating insights that are significant, seminal, sophisticated or subtle. Instead Fascism throve on its magpie borrowings: appealing to Social Darwinism and eugenics, balancing racism and nationalism, nodding towards the corporate state and bowing to the *Führerprinzip*. In tying this bundle together, it showed an acute dependence on charismatic leadership in order to pull the whole thing in line on the basis of mass propaganda techniques, in a way that the dictatorships of the 1930s graphically exemplify.

The defeat of Fascism can be seen as the crucial event of the mid twentieth century. This defeat had an important economic dimension, a starkly significant political dimension, a cataclysmically bloody military dimension, and a deeply poignant human and social dimension. But did it have an intellectual dimension that was at all comparable?

In this respect, I suggest that the demise of Communism, much more recently, raises more interesting questions. For although the Soviet system is undoubtedly not only dead but discredited, it may be premature nonetheless to talk comprehensively about the death of

Marxism, still less the end of history. Indeed this perspective defines the rest of what I have to say about ideology.

The central issue can be put in a very simple way. Some may think it simplistic but I will at least claim that it is simple: how do big ideas get into politics? This poses in the most general way a question which has fascinated me as a working historian for thirty years. What we can call Naïve Intellectualism proposes a model by which great thinkers – and we all know who they are – sit on mountain tops and generate great thoughts, which they then fatefully inscribe into big books, and there is then a process of dissemination, and disciples come along and clutch these great books and read them, and then this leads, given the passage of time, to a process whereby these ideas achieve their implementation.

One classic statement of this view comes in the closing passage of Keynes's *magnum opus*, *The General Theory*, where he asks: is the fulfilment of these ideas a visionary hope?

> the ideas of economists and political philosophers, both when they are right and when they are wrong, are more powerful than is commonly understood. Indeed the world is ruled by little else. Practical men, who believe themselves to be quite exempt from any intellectual influences, are usually the slaves of some defunct economist. Madmen in authority, who hear voices in the air, are distilling their frenzy from some academic scribbler of a few years back. I am sure that the power of vested interests is vastly exaggerated compared with the gradual encroachment of ideas. . . . soon or late it is ideas not vested interests which are dangerous for good or evil.[1]

This is, of course, a canonical statement, boldly delivered. I think it could be argued that Keynes's view was rather more subtle than this passage perhaps allows; but we can leave such subtleties aside for present purposes.

There is certainly an irony in the reception of his own doctrine. The so-called golden age of economic growth in Western Europe and North America, say, from 1945 to 1973, is often known as the Keynesian Era. In the light of Keynes's own hopes for his ideas, we might see it as a validation of those hopes. Certainly his name became synonymous with government management of the economy, especially through what became known as 'fine tuning' and fiscal means of regulating consumer demand; it became synonymous, too, at least in Britain, with a process pejoratively known as 'stop–go' regulation of the economy via the use of interest rates; and it became synonymous, above all, with a policy of supposed budget deficits – the 'tax-and-spend' era, the horrors of which we have heard so much about in recent years.

Yet none of this finds warrant in the writings of the historical Keynes. No wonder he commented on one gathering of economists, towards the end of his life, that he was 'the only non-Keynesian there'! He didn't believe that you could regulate the economy through regulating consumer demand; he said, if anything, it had to be done via public investment. He didn't believe in stop–go and the use of interest rates; interest rates ought to be kept permanently low, according to the *General Theory*. He didn't, above all, believe in simply running budget deficits; the ordinary budget, he said, ought to be balanced year by year. So, here is Keynes, after his death achieving a posthumous accolade (which admittedly later turned sour) by finding himself in the position of an academic scribbler whose ideas were very imperfectly realized in real politics.

My point is not to claim that this process is peculiar to Keynes, nor even to blame subsequent Keynesians for corrupting Keynes. My point is that the ideological distortion of doctrine is in fact almost inevitable. It is a part of the historical process by which doctrines acquire and exert influence and we ought to reconcile ourselves to that idea.

There seems to me to be an instructive comparison here with Marxism, which it is worth exploring at some length. This is especially so because 'vulgar Marxism', as we tend to call it these days, is associated with a determinism of material forces (or what Keynes was calling vested interests) just as what we can call 'vulgar Keynesianism' supposes the triumph of ideas in some more abstract way. Now this raises a very general problem for any political project: how to locate a constituency for a particular agenda. On this issue, I suggest that Marxism offers not one but two very different perspectives.

The first perspective is a historical perspective and is an insight on which we all draw. If we identify an ideology as those beliefs and values that serve the interests of particular groups or classes, we are looking at the instrumental or positional way in which particular ideas can be analysed.

At a homely level, this is what we might call the Mandy Rice Davies problem. Though many older people may immediately sense the allusion, perhaps I ought to open it out by recalling that in the early 1960s Mandy Rice Davies, a woman of striking looks and personality, made herself into a famous oracle on the strength of an appearance in the witness box in a matter connected with the Profumo affair. It was solemnly put to her by a bewigged barrister that what she revealed was contradicted by his embarrassed client, Lord Astor, and that Lord Astor said something completely different: to which Mandy Rice Davies simply responded, 'Well, he would, wouldn't he?'

It was one of those great simplifying remarks that immediately command assent and thereby establish their own status. Perhaps we can use it as a convenient label, therefore, for the process by which we know that there is simply no puzzle in explaining why certain people profess particular propositions, which claim truth, or claim generality, or claim disinterestedness, or claim morality – well, they would, wouldn't they?

Let me introduce another figure into my intellectual pantheon, alongside Mandy Rice Davies, at this point: Vladimir Ilyich Lenin. His trenchant question, of course, was 'who, whom?' It was to ask, in any situation, not so much *what* people were formally purporting to do or professing to believe, but *who* was superior to *whom* in the power relations between them. The inference, of course, was that this would explain all.

Indeed it has been a staple of the Marxist tradition, proceeding in this way, to 'unmask' ideologies. All ideologies? No, other people's ideologies. Admittedly, there have been interesting variants. Not all Marxists have been vulgar materialists, ready to dismiss ideologies held by the 'wrong' classes simply as examples of 'false consciousness'. The more subtle approach of Gramsci, for example, has fruitfully dwelt on the 'hegemony' of a dominant ideology in society as a whole, looking at its success in winning acquiescence even from groups who do not directly benefit from it.

Yet the real difficulty for Marxist analysis surely comes in accounting for Marxism itself. Is socialism or communism just another ideology, serving another set of vested interests, legitimating another self-interested political project? Yet we do not find Marxists characteristically telling us this. That is, in this instance, they refuse to ask, or decline to press, Lenin's question, 'who, whom?' On the whole, we don't find that Marxism has been concerned with unmasking the grandiloquent pretensions to justice, to equity, to the end of exploitation, which were the professed claims of Marxist parties and movements.

Here is the fracture line between what we can call Marxism as history, which ought to ask those questions even of itself, and Marxism as prophecy, to which we will now turn.

For the other perspective that comes from Marxism can truly be called prophetic. Marx's vision was of a qualitative break between history and prophecy. On the one side stands what he called the history of hitherto existing societies, which of course was as class struggles; and, on the other side, stands the future society, towards which he pointed, which would embody the end of exploitation. And Marxism claims special exemption for socialism as ideology because, within capitalism, the proletariat alone can act as a 'universal class' standing for universal interests, rather than merely sectional interests or vested interests, because it alone would have no interest except the universal interest.

This concept of a universal class, of course, was derived by Marx from Hegel. And Marx, in a way that is illuminating about the nature of the doctrine of Marxism, self-consciously cast about to find his universal class at a particular moment in his own thinking. A further substantial quotation may be justified, alongside that from Keynes, in indicating an equally revealing pattern of thought on Marx's part. It is significant that, though their answers are so different, they both proceed by posing an essentially similar question about the role of social agency in realizing a particular agenda. In 1843, when he was living in Paris, Marx addressed himself to this problem and came up with his answer.

Where, then, is the *positive* possibility of German emancipation? Answer: In the formation of a class with *radical chains*, a class in civil society that is not of civil society, a class that is the dissolution of all classes, a sphere of society having a universal character because of its universal suffering and claiming no particular right because no particular wrong but *unqualified wrong* is perpetrated on it; a sphere that can invoke no traditional title but only a human title which does not partially oppose the consequences but totally opposes the premises of the German political system; a sphere, finally, that cannot emancipate itself without emancipating itself from all the other spheres of society thereby emancipating them; a sphere, in short, that is the complete loss of humanity and can only redeem itself through the total redemption of humanity. This dissolution of society as a particular class is the *proletariat*.[2]

The proletariat is identified in this way, not on the basis of any empirical analysis about the actual working class as they existed at this time in Britain – still less in Germany, where nothing like his sort of proletariat really existed at all. This is an all-or-nothing approach. It is not the positive qualifications of the proletariat, it is their paradoxical lack of qualifications, which – turned inside-out in this Hegelian reasoning – gives Marx his answer. It is a philosophical solution to the problem of identifying a universal class.

It had little to do with actual labour movements as they arose, particularly in Britain in the first instance, and then later in other West European countries. Yet they, with all their natural flaws and virtues, were conscripted as carriers of an ideology of Marxism which they adapted to their own purposes. That is to say, they remained ensnared in history.

The point can perhaps be indicated, though hardly adequately substantiated, by a thumb-nail sketch of the history of Marxism as ideology. At least four distinct stages in its propagation can be identified, as different historical possibilities successively opened up – and were successively foreclosed.

In the first place, in Western Europe, which ought, of course, to have been ripe for socialism if Marx's analysis was correct, Marxism indeed found its champions. But actual social democratic parties, though professedly Marxist, opted for incremental strategies in practice rather than revolution, and did so often with bourgeois allies and after great fratricidal soul-searching. One thinks particularly of the SPD in Germany, where there were famous set-piece battles over 'revisionism' – what Bernstein said against Kautsky, what Kautsky said against Rosa Luxemburg – all really trying to reinterpret the doctrine in order to make it fit a changing political reality. Even in the British Labour Party we have had our own pallid and belated version of the same thing in the late twentieth century with the two historic attempts to remove Clause 4 of the party constitution, committing it to the public ownership of means of production: the first attempt, of course, unsuccessful under Hugh Gaitskell, the second attempt successful under Tony Blair. Parties throughout Western Europe, then, even when claiming nominal Marxist credentials, have adopted quite other political strategies in practice.

Secondly, in Eastern Europe, notably Russia, we see that there was indeed an opportunity for revolution which was seized by Lenin and by Trotsky. We see the Bolshevik experiment put in place from 1917, forcing the pace from above, in a process during which Lenin and Trotsky notoriously fell out. Trotsky accused Lenin at one point of substituting the party for the proletariat and Trotsky himself later invested his own hopes in what he called 'permanent revolution', that is to say a process of ongoing revolution. Although it had started in Russia, a primitve society which was exactly the wrong place for it, revolution would nonetheless spread to the advanced capitalist societies of Britain and the United States, which would become the true focus of a world revolution. Hence Trotsky's poignant comment that history was unwinding her skein from the wrong end.

In the third world – our own third stage – we can see the immense ideological success of Marxism in generating ostensible support. We can see this ideology projected onto peasant societies in the context of nationalist revolutions, especially in China. We can see, too, the paradoxical way that Marxism was seized upon, identifying Western exploitation, yet often legitimating the role of Marxist nationalist elites who became leaders of those revolutions precisely because they themselves were Westernized. For example, between the wars, Ho Chi Minh had spent time in Paris – I believe he was working as a chef – which was in that sense an important *hors-d'oeuvre* to his later political career.

Finally (for this is not an exhaustive list) I will invoke everything that we mean by '1968', the last great resurgence of Marxism in the West. Disappointed in its hopes of enlisting the European or North American proletariat, disillusioned with the 'actually existing social-ism' represented by Soviet Communism, dislocated from the anti-imperialist struggles of faraway peasant societies, Marxism was still an ideology in search of a universal class. Perhaps it is not surprising that some sophisticated Western Marxists, faced with these unpromising historical circumstances, were so desperate to find the long-sought universal class that they heard the rattle of its radical chains in their own universities. Marxism thus turned to the students as its last, best hope. On this experiment I make no further comment.

The point is that – even here, especially here – Marxism can still yield *historical* insights. It can do so if we relentlessly ask 'who, whom?' in all of these cases, exploring them with rather more sophistication than I have been able to do in my thumb-nail sketch. But Marxism *as prophecy* has a sorry record. Our conclusion here must be that there was no class that was the privileged bearer of a uniquely liberating ideology – no social group that was uniquely correct, no sure road to scientific socialism, or any of the other things promised and prophesied by Marxist doctrine.

Conversely, it is not a decisive 'unmasking' to identify the ideological purchase of ideas, that is to say why any ideas are selectively appropriated or why they are subject to ideological distortion in the process. This is surely *one* pertinent aspect for us as historians in understanding the reception of any doctrine, and it does not pre-empt judgement on its intellectual scientific or moral status. For it must be the case that someone can hold a self-interested belief that is also 'true' or 'correct'. If we find a Zionist insisting that the Nazi Holocaust really happened, it is not enough to respond, 'Well, he would, wouldn't he?'

Not only is it clear that the process of 'unmasking', as a staple of the whole Marxist tradition of political analysis, presupposes that there are irreducible interests: more broadly, 'unmasking' presupposes that there are irreducible motives of a unitary character. In the Marxist model, these are defined as class interest, so that, once we have unmasked the contending ideologies, underneath we will find that they reveal a clash between different classes.

There are, however, other models here, equally available to such a process of unmasking, until we strip everything down to a supposedly irreducible level (and then stop). We could, if we were following Bentham, relentlessly attribute everything to his rather reductionist axioms of self-interest, to the maximization of pleasure and the avoidance of pain, and when we get to that level unerringly identify these as the irreducible motives. If we follow Machiavelli, we can follow a process of unmasking whereby we eventually come down to power and fear – again intuitively identified as irreducible motives. If we follow Freud, we find a similar process of unmasking, so that we will inevitably discover, no matter how it may be dressed up, that it is actually all about sex.

Now I am not saying that these influential thinkers are wrong, still less that that these are implausible motives. But it is reductionist to keep unmasking in this way until we reach some presupposed, selective motive, which we can then triumphantly expose as the *real* motive or the *real* explanation for whatever is going on. It is this whole procedure, I suggest, that is tautologous and illegitimate.

If so, a rather important conclusion follows. Just as the intellectual-ist confidence in the primacy of ideas is naïve, so also is the attempt to reduce the value of ideas to the status of their bearers, which is the characteristic Marxist fallacy (though a fallacy not confined to Marxism). Hence, while we should continue to ask the Lenin question ('who, whom?') because it is indeed a very good question to ask, we should also continue to make another equally pertinent inquiry ('what, what?'), which it is tempting to call the George III question. We need to ask, in short, about the actual content of the ideas that we are dealing with here; and by asking both questions at once, or at least successively, we might get a little further than by only asking one of them because of our presuppositions about the answers.

Above all, it seems to me the twentieth century shows that there is no universal class capable of transcending history, understood as the history of hitherto existing society. In the First World War one of the songs that the troops sang was:

It's the same the whole world over,
It's the poor what gets the blame;
It's the rich what gets the pleasure,
Ain't it all a bloomin' shame?

This tragic vision, I suggest, is something that is part of Marx's vision too (in a necessarily colloquial form). This is one reason why the so-called death of Marxism is not the end of history as Francis Fukuyama famously proclaimed at the beginning of the 1990s. There is plenty of history left to happen – in fact, rather too much history for some people's good or comfort, in a world that is riven by ethnic conflict, by gross and increasing inequalities both within nations and between them, and a looming environmental crisis. Just because Communism is over, don't let us trivialize this, by talking about the end of history.

What we don't need is Marxism as prophecy: as one big answer, hedgehog-style. Its paradigm of revelation and salvation is almost comically dependent on secularizing Christian doctrine, and surely rests on a misguided expectation of a qualitative shift or break within history, when an inherently flawed and sinful world gives way to the promised kingdom of heaven on earth.

Instead, I would suggest we rely upon the uniformitarian assumption. I am drawing here of course on the idea introduced by the great early nineteenth-century geologist Charles Lyell. It may be no coincidence that the 'catastrophist' views of geology that he contested – we would probably call them 'creationist' today – were themselves imbued with the notion of direct providential intervention as a means of explaining the shaping and reshaping of the world, rather than relying on the long, slow processes of natural history. Lyell said that we were much safer to rest on the assumption that the same processes that we can observe at work in the present were also at work in the past and will also be at work in the future. This does not, of course, rule out the sudden occurrence of earthquakes, the eruption of volcanoes and other untoward events of that kind.

Historically, then, I am definitely a uniformitarian. That is why I think that Marxism as history can still be made to yield insights for us; whereas Marxism as prophecy has turned out to be delusive. This is not, I think, a static or inherently conservative view but a warrant for incremental change rather than any transformative doctrine. So I end in my wishy-washy, Cambridge liberal way, rather like E.M. Forster, giving two cheers for democracy – and two cheers also for the twenty-first century as the century of the fox which has seen the demise of the hedgehog.

Notes and References

1 J.M. Keynes, *The General Theory of Employment, Interest and Money* (London, 1936) p. 383.
2 Karl Marx, 'Toward the critique of Hegel's Philosophy of Law' (1843), in *Writings of the Young Marx on Philosophy and Society*, translated and edited by Loyd H. Easton and Kurt H. Guddat (New York: Anchor Books, 1967), pp. 262–3.

TIM BLANNING

Culture at the Start of the
New Millennium

As the second millennium drew to a close, world culture seemed to be dominated by two conflicting trends. On the one hand, there was the inexorable spread of American consumer culture, ensuring that everywhere in the developed world the same artefacts and services could be bought. Indeed, the presence of branded goods was itself a qualification of developed status – if Big Macs, Nike trainers, Tommy Hilfiger sportswear, MTV or CNN were not available, one had to be somewhere very primitive. As Theodore Levitt of the Harvard Business School remarked in his seminal essay of 1983, 'The Globalization of Markets': 'The world's needs and desires have been irrevocably homogenized.'[1] On the other hand, 'high culture' had moved to the opposite extreme of subjectivism, exemplified by the English artist Tracey Emin, who put on public display such intimate possessions as her rumpled bed and soiled underwear.

This apparent contradiction may be less of a paradox than it seems, for Tracey Emin attracted huge attention from the media and high prices for her creations. Although exceptionally adept at managing publicity, she was no isolated phenomenon, as was demonstrated by the phenomenal success of the Tate Modern gallery, which opened in the millennial year and attracted 120,000 visitors during its first three days.

It seems even less of a paradox if it is placed in historical context. In this essay I shall argue that the culture of Europe during the past three centuries or so has been dominated by a dialectical relationship between two cultural paradigms – the culture of passion and the

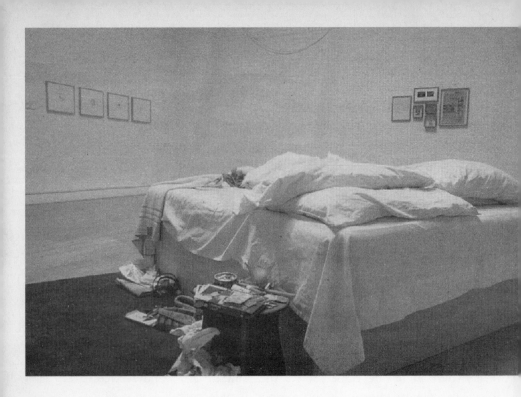

Tracey Emin, 'My Bed', 1998 (*photograph by Stephen White; reproduced by permission of Jay Jopling/White Cube, London*)

culture of reason. It is not my intention to be exclusive or reductionist – there are plenty of other ways to conceptualize modern culture – but this does seem to me to be one valid way. I am also aware, of course, that this conflict dates back to the dawn of human history, not least because it is rooted in human nature.

I have chosen two visual images to illustrate the culture of passion. The first is *The Dream of Philip II*, painted in 1578–9 by Doménikos Theotokópoulos, better known as 'El Greco', although he was a Venetian subject born on the island of Crete. Also known as *Allegory of the Holy League*, it shows Philip II of Spain, the Pope and the Doge of Venice giving thanks to the Almighty for His assistance in defeating the Ottoman Turks at the Battle of Lepanto in 1571. However, it is very much more than a victory celebration; indeed, it is nothing less than a depiction of Man's relation to God, underpinned by St Paul's injunction in his epistle to the Philippians: 'At the name of Jesus, every knee should bow, of things in heaven and things on earth and things in hell.' El Greco's mystic vision comes from deep inside

El Greco, 'The Dream of Philip II',
c. 1577 (*AKG London*)

Giovanni Lorenzo Bernini,
'Ecstasy of Saint Teresa of Avila',
1644–7 (*AKG London/Erich Lessing*)

himself, from an introspective world of dreams and the subconscious, yielding an image which is suffused with movement, colour and emotion. Juxtaposing penitence and sin, life and death, salvation and damnation, its agenda is essentially *jenseitig* (privileging the other side of the grave), as it advertises the superior reality of the transcendental realm. It also has a strong erotic charge, whether in the vaginal gape of hell or in the fluttering limbs of the nude putti and lightly clad androgynous angels as they wriggle upwards. A mannerist master-piece, it transgresses every classical canon.

This erotic element is even more pronounced in my second illustration, Gianlorenzo Bernini's multi-media *The Ecstasy of Saint Teresa of Ávila* in the Cornaro Chapel of Santa Maria della Vittoria in Rome, created between 1645 and 1652. As members of the Cornaro family look on from their box, as if in a theatre, Saint Teresa experiences the vision she described as follows:

> One day an Angel of surpassing beauty appeared to me in a vision. He held in his hand a long spear whose tip glowed as if it were on fire. This he thrust several times into my heart so that it penetrated to the very depth of my being. The pain was so real that I cried out several times, and yet it was also so unutterably sweet that I could not wish to be spared it. Life can offer no joy which could give me greater satisfaction. And when the Angel withdrew his spear I remained in a state of total love for God.[2]

It would be difficult to think of a better illustration of Sigmund Freud's dictum that 'a dream is a *disguised* fulfilment of a *suppressed* wish'. It should also be sufficient warning to anyone naïve enough to suppose that, just because Christianity preaches against the sins of the flesh, religion and sexuality are opposed to each other. On the contrary.

By the time Bernini created this extraordinary expression of his own sensual vision of religious experience, the opposing cultural paradigm had been given a potent new articulation by the French philosopher René Descartes. His sombre portrait by Frans Hals provides as stark a contrast with the sensuous world of El Greco or Bernini as it is possible to imagine. In *Discourse on Method* of 1637, Descartes provided the conceptual tools which would bring the

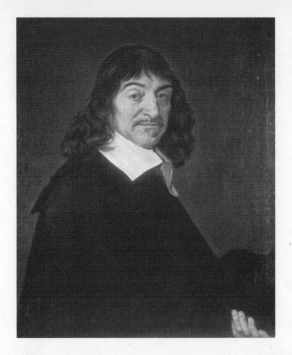

Frans Hals, portrait of René Descartes, *c.* 1640 (*AKG London/Erich Lessing*)

mystical clouds of Philip II or Saint Theresa down to earth – mainly in the form of showers of H_2O. The most deflationary was his advocacy of systematic doubt: 'to place our knowledge on foundations which are genuinely secure, we must doubt all of our beliefs, retaining them only if they are absolutely indisputable'. In reassembling the sound parts of the structure that survived, there was only one human faculty that could be trusted – reason. So a fundamental objective of the Cartesian project was 'to lead the mind away from the senses'. The culture which he personified was rational, secular, analytical, atomistic, sceptical, activist and optimistic.

Consequently, Descartes and his successors were able to benefit from a cultural revolution which was just beginning to get underway when Descartes died in 1650. This was the emergence of the public sphere, a new kind of cultural space in which private individuals came together to exchange information, ideas and opinions. Many and deep-rooted were its origins, but the most important was the expansion of literacy which spread the ability to communicate

Antoine Watteau, 'Shop Sign of the Art Dealer Gersaint', 1720 (*AKG London*)

symbolically beyond the narrow circles of clergy and academics. In the course of the late-seventeenth and eighteenth centuries, the proliferation of books, periodicals and newspapers created a 'republic of letters', in which authors and readers joined in a common pursuit of truth, guided only by their reason. It was a process greatly assisted by the simultaneous expansion of population, markets and cities. Whereas access to the official culture of the established regimes was governed by its purpose, namely to advertise the power and legitimacy of the sovereigns, access to the public sphere was open to anyone who could pay. The representational culture of the old regime reached its apogee with Louis XIV's great cultural complex at Versailles, although by the time the old king died in 1715 after seventy-two years on the throne, it was beginning to look frayed at the edges.

The transition was expressed visually with special delicacy by Antoine Watteau, in his painting *The Shop-sign of Gersaint* (1721). Created in the last year of his short life (1684–1721) to hang outside the art-gallery of his eponymous friend, this is surely the finest advertisement of any age. *The Shop-sign of Gersaint* is also revealing because of what it was: a sign for a shop in Paris. The paintings on the wall are all commodities and the chief characters are customers. Indeed the shop-sign itself was for sale, serving its original purpose for only a few weeks before being bought by Watteau's patron Jean de Julienne. Its commercial nature was emphasized by its subsequent proliferation in the form of an engraving made in 1732, which was how it came to the attention and then into the possession of Frederick the Great of Prussia. Watteau's familiar technique for imparting an erotic charge to his painting, by juxtaposing the nudes in his paintings with fully dressed observers, does not alter the fact that what is being represented in *The Shop-sign of Gersaint* is a commercial transaction. It is not a critique: Watteau was a close friend of Gersaint, was living in his house at the time and painted this sign as an act of friendship. However, it does depict an important transitional moment, poignantly caught as the woman stepping in from the street pauses to look at the portrait of Louis XIV being packed away. Her companion extends his hand to beckon her on, indicating that there is no point in dwelling on yesterday's man.

The contrast between the two cultures can also be illustrated by comparing two libraries. The primary purpose of the Court Library in Vienna, built by Johann Bernhard Fischer von Erlach, was to represent (in the sense of 'making present') the power and glory of its patron, the Holy Roman Emperor Charles VI. It is not designed primarily as a room in which books could be stored and read, as most of the space is devoted to frescoes and bas-reliefs celebrating the achievements of the Habsburg dynasty or to imposing architectural features. By contrast, Wright's circulating library exists to provide as many books as possible for as many readers as possible, thus generating as large a profit as possible for the owner. Significantly, this commercial library was to be found in London, whose population, wealth and liberty led to the development of a public sphere of exceptional size and activity. Together with the expansion of publishing to meet the extra demand and the consequent reduction of the cost of books thanks to economies of scale, the proliferation of libraries led to a new way of reading. Because there were now so many more books available, both the readers and the way in which they read changed. When few titles were produced in small and expensive

1s, the texts were read again and again, mainly for the purposes
otion, instruction and edification. The typical readers were the
s with their breviaries, the lawyers with their handbooks or the
ul with their bibles. In short, they read intensively. Once there
were thousands of titles available, produced in larger and cheaper
editions, new kinds of readers joined in, looking for topical
information, practical advice and recreation, reading books once and
then discarding them. In short, they read extensively.

This 'reading revolution' of the eighteenth century did not pass
unnoticed by contemporaries. This was very much a perceived change
and, moreover, one which was seen to have implications for other
fields of human activity. The Parisian journalist Louis-Sébastien
Mercier wrote in 1787: 'Ten times more people are reading today than
a hundred years ago. Today you can see a maid in a basement or a
lackey in an ante-room reading a pamphlet. They are reading in
almost every class of society, and so much the better. They should be
reading even more. The nation which reads is a nation which carries
in its breast a special and felicitous force, which can challenge and
frustrate despotism.' When the old regime collapsed two years later, it
seemed to many contemporaries that it was a revolution driven by
reason. Descartes had believed that his critical methodology would
consolidate the established divine and terrestrial order, but his
successors could see more clearly that reason was both Prometheus
and Proteus. In his *Historical and Critical Dictionary* of 1697, Pierre
Bayle found a particularly graphic simile to express its corrosive
quality, comparing it 'to one of those apothecary's powders that, after
consuming the oozing flesh of a wound, begins to eat away the healthy
flesh, and then rots the bones all the way through to the marrow'.[3]

The French Revolution very quickly celebrated the apotheosis of
reason and the rejection of the past. As its main ideologue, the Abbé
Sieyès, maintained: 'the alleged "truths" of history have no more
reality than the alleged "truths" of religion'.[4] Turning their back self-
consciously on the past, the revolutionaries believed they could start
afresh with a *tabula rasa*, inscribing on it a rational new order of
universal application. The climax was the formal worship of reason at
a ceremony held at the Cathedral of Notre Dame (renamed the
Temple of Reason) on 10 November 1793 to celebrate 'the triumph
that Reason has just won over the prejudices of eighteen centuries'.[5]

The Court Library in Vienna, built 1723–53 (*AKG London/Erich Lessing*)

Wright's Circulating Library (*Bodleian Library, University of Oxford; shelfmark Douce Portfolio 139 [808]*)

'A la philosophie': Festival of the Supreme Being, 10 November 1793
(© *Collection Viollet*)

In the following month an opera entitled *The Festival of Reason* was performed at the Opéra, with music by Grétry. A chorus of newly enlightened villagers sing to their priest:

O Divinity of every age!
Whom we can adore without blushing,
Reason! Whom our less sensible ancestors
Left to groan so long under the yoke of error;
Be the guide of our country,
Purge it of all abuses.
And inspire in the hearts of our compatriots
A love of order and virtue.[6]

By the time those words were sung, the Terror was giving the reign of reason a bad name. To paraphrase Madame Roland's cry about Liberty, as she ascended the scaffold, 'Oh Reason! What crimes are committed in thy name!' Yet this was not a sudden reaction. The culture of passion exemplified by El Greco or Bernini had never been extinguished by the apparently triumphant – and certainly triumphalist – march of reason. At the very moment of the Enlightenment's greatest successes during the middle decades of the eighteenth century, hostile forces began to stir. It was in 1749, the year before the publication of Montesquieu's *De l'esprit des lois*, that Rousseau experienced his conversion on the road to Vincennes, when he suddenly realized that civilization did not make humankind more free or more moral. Especially in Germany, his privileging of emotion over reason found a ready response. Increasingly alienated by the arrogance of the French, they attacked the very foundations of the Enlightenment's cosmopolitan rationalism. The Prussian Pietist Johann Georg Hamann asked angrily: 'What is this much lauded reason with its universality, infallibility . . . certainty, over-weening claims, but an *ens rationis*, a stuffed dummy . . . endowed with divine attributes?'[7] A defining moment was the journey to Strassburg by Goethe in March 1770, at the age of twenty-one, to study law at the university. It was there that he had an epiphany, comparable to Rousseau's moment of revelation, when he looked at the great cathedral and saw, not the Gothic monstrosity derided by enlightened taste but an object of unique beauty. It was a revelation he shared with the world in an essay entitled 'Concerning German Architecture', dedicated to Erwin von Steinbach, the building's main architect. Here he used his new enthusiasm for the Gothic to preach a new aesthetic *credo*. Any idea that beauty could be found by joining schools, adopting principles or following rules was emphatically rejected: they were so many chains enslaving insight and energy.

The ghastly good taste, harmony and purity demanded by classical aesthetics did violence to nature's untamed spontaneity. In the essay's key passage Goethe defined his alternative: 'The only true art is characteristic art. If its influence arises from deep, harmonious, independent feeling, from feeling peculiar to itself, oblivious, yes, ignorant of everything foreign, then it is whole and living, whether it be born from crude savagery or cultured sentiment.'[8] The crucial adjective is 'characteristic' (*karakteristische*), by which Goethe meant art which grows naturally and spontaneously from the culture within which it is produced, not something that has been imitated. In the case of Strassburg Cathedral, it was not only characteristic art, it was

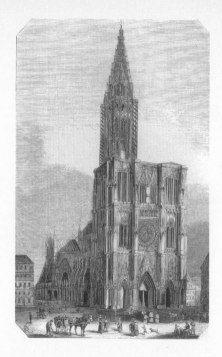

Strassburg Cathedral, 1845 (*AKG London*)

also art that was characteristically German. It had been produced on German soil 'in authentically German times' (*in echter deutscher Zeit*) and only gained in stature by virtue of being treated with contempt by the Italians or the French.[9]

From the insights of individuals such as Rousseau and Goethe, a new world view was created. The 'romantic revolution' opposed emotion to reason, faith to scepticism, intuition to logic, subjectivity to objectivity, historicism to natural law, poetry to prose. In the view of the romantics, the Enlightenment and its scientific method had analysed and analysed until the world lay around them in a dismantled, atomized, and meaningless heap. So it was a common accusation that the Enlightenment 'could explain everything, but understand nothing'. The *philosophes* committed the fault of Madame de Warens, Rousseau's lover, of whom he wrote in *The Confessions*: 'instead of listening to her heart, which gave her good counsel, she listened to her reason, which gave her bad'.[10] It was in this spirit that Heinrich von Kleist sneered that Sir Isaac Newton, the personification

Francisco Goya, 'The Sleep of Reason Begets Monsters',
1797–8 (*AKG London*)

of the scientific revolution, would see in a girl's breast only a crooked
line and in her heart nothing more interesting than its cubic capacity,
while William Blake proclaimed that 'Art is the Tree of Life. Science
is the Tree of Death'. In the place of the arid abstractions of
rationalism, the romantics called for a remystification of the world.
Against the natural aesthetic laws of neo-classicism, they opposed the
spontaneity and originality of the inner light of genius. As the greatest
of the romantic painters, Caspar David Friedrich, put it: ' The painter
should not just paint what he sees in front of him, but also what he
sees inside himself. But if he should see nothing inside himself, then
he should stop painting what he sees in front of him. Otherwise his
pictures would become mere screens behind which one expects to find
only the sick or even the dead.'[11] To gain access to what really
mattered, the romantics believed, reason and its main instrument –
the word – were not so much inadequate as misleading, instilling a
false sense of precision and clarity. If nature was not an inert mass,
governed by the blind, mechanical Newtonian laws, but a vibrant

organism pulsating with life, then it could be understood only by allowing the other human faculties to resume their rightful place. It was an indication of their rejection of the Enlightenment's rationalism that they turned its central metaphor – light – on its head. 'The cold light of day' was rejected as superficial and in its place was enthroned 'the wonder-world night'. Is the owl perched on the artist's shoulder in Goya's *The Sleep of Reason Begets Monsters* a monster to be feared, or is it not rather the Owl of Minerva, the symbol of wisdom, who 'flies only at dusk'? From Novalis (the *nom de plume* of Friedrich von Hardenberg) and his *Hymns to the Night* to Richard Wagner and *Tristan and Isolde*, the night was celebrated as 'the mother of all that is true and beautiful'.

So the triumph of reason proclaimed by the French Revolutionaries lasted no longer than their own chimerical regime. Yet the wider process of modernization, of which the French Revolution was a mere symptom, could not be arrested. The spread of literacy, the improvement of physical communications, the accelerating pace of scientific innovation, the rapid increase in population, urbanization, the expansion of the public sphere – just to list a selection of the forces at work – combined to promote a sense of sustained secular progress. Once again, technological change seemed to herald emancipation from more than reliance on the quadruped or Shank's pony. As Friedrich Harkort, a German industrialist, put it in 1847: 'The locomotive is the hearse that will carry absolutism and feudalism to the graveyard.'[12] It was in the same year that Adolph Menzel painted the Berlin–Potsdam railway and a year later that Germany (and continental Europe) was engulfed by a wave of revolutions.

On the other hand, the dislocation caused by industrialization and urbanization convinced many observers that the poor were becoming more wretched, more numerous, and more dangerous. This did not mean that all artists became socialists, but it did mean that a growing number of them chose the material conditions of the here and now as their central concern. It was no accident that the literary genre best suited to the new direction, first known as 'realism' and later as 'naturalism', was the novel, for the world of the modern city was prosaic rather than poetic. In works such as Dickens's *Oliver Twist* (1837–9), Gustav Freytag's *Profit and Loss* (1855), Dostoevsky's *Crime and Punishment* (1866), or the twenty volumes of Emile Zola's

Adolph Menzel, 'The Berlin–Potsdam Railway' (*AKG London*)

'Rougon-Macquart' cycle (1870–93), the wonderful variety of commercialized urban society was usually less apparent than its attendant squalor and tension. This was the realm of anomie, that sense of moral rootlessness which the French sociologist Emile Durkheim identified as the essence of the human condition in the industrialized world.

Also naturally suited for capturing contemporary reality was painting, which found an articulate spokesman for the new approach in Gustave Courbet, as well as a wonderfully gifted practitioner. Among his trenchant observations on the nature of his art were 'painting is an essentially *concrete* art and can only consist of the presentation of *real and existing things*', and the quintessentially anti-romantic jibe: 'show me an angel and I'll paint it!'[13] Although never a propagandist, Courbet was very much a man of the left, a republican and supporter of the revolutionary Commune of 1871, who paid for his beliefs by spending two years in prison and the rest of his life in exile. Together with Jean-François Millet and Edouard Manet he represented, as it were, the 'heroic' phase of realism, all funerals, firing-squads, hunched peasant women, and horny-handed sons of toil. Shown the way forward by Manet, in the 1870s a younger generation of painters lightened both the mood and their palettes. The 'impressionists', notably Camille Pissarro, Edgar Degas, Alfred Sisley, Claude Monet, Pierre Auguste Renoir and Georges Seurat, moved from the place of work to the place of recreation – to the garden, seaside, racetrack, dancehall, theatre. Their dazzling exploration of light in every conceivable shape and form were to become *the* great artistic success story of the following century, both in auction-rooms and on chocolate boxes. This realist trend was underpinned by a positivist belief in the natural sciences. As Zola wrote of the Salon of 1866: 'The wind blows in the direction of science. Despite ourselves, we are pushed towards the exact study of facts and things.'[14] As technological advance was piled on technological advance, especially in the field of communications, and as the publication of *On the Origin of Species* by Charles Darwin in 1859 seemed to deliver the *coup de grâce* to revealed religion, the disenchantment of the world seemed complete. Moreover, it was accompanied by the allied triumph of liberalism. This was the period when Italy and Germany were unified and when liberals took control in one state after another (even in the multinational Habsburg Empire).

In his novel *The Stomach Paris*, published in 1873, Zola put the following words into the mouth of Claude Lankier, who points first at the iron and glass structure of the recently erected central market – Les Halles – and then at the neighbouring medieval church Saint Eustache, predicting: 'This one will kill that one, for iron will kill stone.' He was not the first materialist to be deluded by the shadows on the wall of the cave: Les Halles were demolished in the 1970s, but Saint Eustache still stands. There were plenty of contemporaries who could appreciate the limitations of Courbet's or Zola's *Weltanschauung*. That was one reason why the musicians, who had never abandoned romanticism, came to be so very influential on the other branches of the arts during the second half of the nineteenth century. Leading the field was Richard Wagner, not only because of the unique power of his creations but also because of the cogency of his critique of the whole modern project. He wrote to his old friend Ernst Benedikt Kietz from his Swiss exile in 1851: 'My entire political outlook no longer consists in anything but the bloodiest hatred of our

Les Halles, Paris (© *Collection Viollet*)

Saint Eustache, *c.* 1895 (*AKG London*)

Gustav Klimt, 'Medicine' (*Galerie Welz, Salzburg*)

entire civilisation, contempt for all that it has produced, and a passionate longing for nature.'[15] No German romantic was more uncompromising in his rejection of reason. His second wife, Cosima, recorded in her diary on 19 April 1873: 'In the morning conversation about the Germans and the French, there is talk of civil war breaking out among our neighbours. "If only we could reach the point of no longer looking to them for our ideas!" R[ichard] says. "How low they have sunk one can see by the fact that they imagine they can get things done by maxims based on reason. As if anything ever comes of reason!" '[16] In Wagner's view, the modern world was utterly perverted by a lust for power and a corresponding rejection of love. In the four-part *The Ring of the Nibelung*, he exposed the consequences, while in its sequel, *Parsifal*, he offered an alternative vision of a new order based on compassion and renunciation of the will.

By the time *The Ring* was first performed at Wagner's own festival-theatre at Bayreuth in 1876, the triumphalist march of industrialization and its positivist culture was beginning to falter. The social tensions created by the long recession beginning in 1873, the eruption of new mass political forces, with socialism, clericalism and anti-Semitism to the fore, ensured that the high-noon of bourgeois liberalism was of short duration. A romantic revival rediscovered the maxims of an earlier generation: in 1888 the 20-year-old French painter Émile Bernard virtually repeated the words of Caspar David Friedrich quoted above when he wrote that the artist should not paint what he sees in front of him but the idea of the thing he sees in his imagination. Similarly, the central tenet of what became known as 'symbolism', as expressed by its main organ *Symbolist* – 'Objectivity is nothing but vain appearance, that I may vary or transform as I wish' – could have been said by any romantic two or three generations earlier. The old romantic obsessions with death, the night, and sex were all back in favour again, nowhere more powerfully than in Gustav Klimt's notorious ceiling paintings for the University of Vienna. What the academics had wanted and expected was a portrayal of the victory of reason, knowledge and enlightenment. What they got was a world turned upside down, in which philosophy is subconscious instinct, justice in 'Jurisprudence' is a cowed and helpless victim of the Law and behind Hygeia, the Greek goddess of health, in 'Medicine' lurk more interesting phenomena than physical fitness and personal hygiene, notably sex and death. This phantasmagoria has much in common with the visions of El Greco or Goya, but it is not a simple case of repetition. European culture has not repeated itself cyclically but has developed dialectically. High-Victorian positivism was not a re-run of the Enlightenment, nor was *fin de siècle* a repetition of romanticism. No romantic would have adopted the radical 'perspect-ivism' of Nietzsche, for example, who did not just privilege subjectivism but denied the very possibility of objectivity: 'So what is truth? A mobile army of metaphors, metonyms, anthropomorphisms – in short an aggregate of human relationships which, poetically and rhetorically heightened, became transposed and elaborate, and which, after protracted popular usage, poses as fixed, canonical, obligatory. Truths are illusions whose illusoriness is overlooked.'[17]

At the turn of the twentieth century, European culture appeared to dissolve into stylistic anarchy. Among the movements in the visual arts, there was the decadent movement, symbolism, syntheticism, neo-impressionism, post-impressionism, constructivism, fauvism,

Antonio Gaudí's *Casa Milá*, built
1906–10 (*AKG London/Hilbich*)

Bauhaus, Dessau (*AKG London*)

Auguste Rodin, 'Balzac',
1897 (*AKG London*)

Constantin Brancusi, 'Sleeping Muse',
c. 1906/10 (*AKG London*; © *ADAGP,
Paris and DACS, London 2002*)

expressionism, cubism, futurism, orphism, neo-plasticism, vorticism, suprematicism, imagism, purism, dadaism, surrealism, and so on. Yet beneath the chaos the dialectical relationship between the culture of passion and the culture of reason · continued. In reaction to the excesses of *fin de siècle* there emerged a general trend towards aesthetic purification. In music, it can be seen (and heard) in Arnold Schoenberg's move from the lush post-Wagnerian orchestration of *Gurrelieder* (begun in 1900) to the atonal austerity of *Five Orchestral Pieces* (1909). In architecture it can be seen in the contrast between Antonio Gaudi's *Casa Milá* (1906–10) and Walter Gropius' Bauhaus (1925–6). In sculpture it can be seen in the contrast between the neo-baroque swirls of Auguste Rodin's *Balzac* (1897–8) and the spare simplicity of Constantin Brancusi's *Sleeping Muse* (1910). In painting it can be seen in the contrast between the voluptuous eroticism of Lovis Corinth's *Salome* (1899) and the chaste linearity of Piet Mondrian's *Composition in Lines* (1916–7). T.S. Eliot spoke for all modernist artists, and not just for writers, when he observed: 'The progress of the artists is a continual self-sacrifice, a continual extinction of personality. Poetry is not the turning loose of emotions but an escape from emotion, not the expression of personality but the escape from personality.'[18] That is a truly Cartesian proposition.

Even after taking account of the wonderful variety of European culture during the first half of the twentieth century, the centre of gravity was definitely located in the culture of reason. As Martin Jay has written, 'aesthetic modernism at mid-century, precisely because of its detachment from concrete social and political practice, came to be taken by many as the appropriate cultural expression of a much larger project of human emancipation.'[19] The association was greatly strengthened by the obtrusive philistinism of fascism in its various forms. If they had not been so sinister, Mussolini's call for 'spiritual imperialism' or Hitler's exhibition of 'degenerate art' would have been risible. They were certainly grim warnings to modernists everywhere, as was the great diaspora of talent from Italy and Germany after 1922 and 1933 respectively. The situation in the Soviet Union was less straightforward. On the one hand, there was Stalin's persecution of avant-garde artists, exemplified by the silencing of Shostakovich in 1936. On the other hand, there were still legions of intellectuals in the

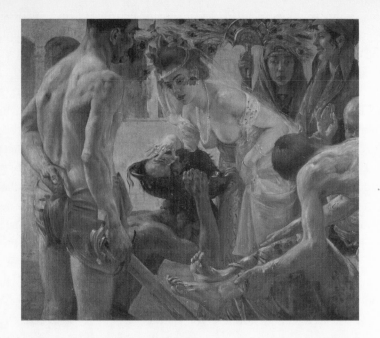

Lovis Corinth, 'Salome', 1900 (*AKG London/Erich Lessing*)

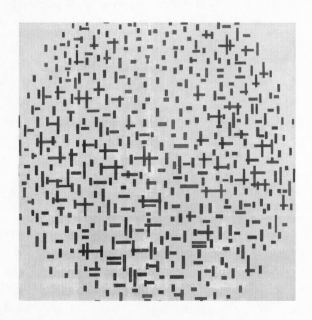

Piet Mondrian, 'Composition in lines', 1916–7 (*AKG London*;
© *Piet Mondrian 2002 Mondrian/Holtzman Trust c/o Beeldrecht,
Hoofddorp & DACS, London*)

West who chose to believe that Stalinism was Marxism, failing to see that it was a perversion of Leninism, which in turn was a perversion of Marxism. Operation Barbarossa in 1941 seemed to confirm the existence of a Manichaean struggle between light and darkness, reason and unreason.

The total victory of 1945 was acclaimed in both West and East as a cultural as well as a military triumph. The discovery of the full horrors of National Socialism engendered a belief in the absolute values of liberalism or communism every bit as self-confident as that entertained by the French Revolutionaries of 1789 or the liberals of the mid-nineteenth century. The collapse of the wartime alliance and prolonged struggle between the two victors in an intense ideological Cold War helped to maintain the triumphalist impetus, as each side noisily proclaimed its own special virtues and the opposition's defects. Of the visual evidence which confirmed the victory of modernism, perhaps the most obtrusive was the rash of skyscrapers, all in the spare, linear, rational 'international style', which mushroomed across the globe. It was also the clearest indication that modernism at last had found a style in which it felt at home. In the nineteenth century, almost every conceivable style had been tried – neo-Gothic, neo-classical, neo-Renaissance, neo-Egyptian, neo-baroque, neo-everything. Heinrich Hübsch actually published a pamphlet in 1828 asking pathetically *In what style should we build?*[20] By the middle of the twentieth century, modernism knew what it wanted. One of its most eloquent spokesmen, Nikolaus Pevsner, regarded this development as 'full of promise', posing the rhetorical question: 'Can we not take it then that the recovery of a true style in the visual arts, one in which once again building rules, and painting and sculpture serve, and one which is obviously representative of character, indicates the return of unity in society too?'[21] A comparison between the wonderfully eclectic Paris Opéra, designed by Charles Garnier and opened in 1875, and the bleak Deutsche Oper (German Opera) in West Berlin, designed by Fritz Bornemann and opened in 1961, makes the point well.

The Deutsche Oper opened on 24 September 1961, just six weeks after the erection of the Berlin Wall had begun. The latter was supposed to make the Eastern Bloc safe for socialism. With the advantage of hindsight, we can see that the system was doomed. Many were the corrosive forces which brought the wall tumbling down just

Opéra, Paris, *c.* 1888 (*AKG London*)

Deutsche Oper, Berlin (*AKG London/Dieter E. Hoppe*)

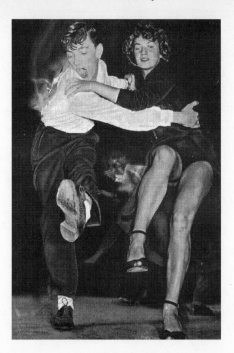

Dancing couple (*from Christian Zentner*, Deutschland 1870 bis heute, *Südwest Verlag, Munich, 1970*)

twenty-eight years later, among them economic failure, the arms race, and the Soviet defeat in Afghanistan, but perhaps the most powerful was advancing communications technology. The evil empires of Hitler, Mussolini and Stalin had benefited from a perfect match between their despotic objectives and the instruments of control available. Without electronic amplification, the radio or the cinema, they could not have cowed so many for so long. By the 1960s, television was eclipsing all other forms of mass media and was proving increasingly difficult to control. The Berlin Wall could keep a people in prison but it could not keep out images of Western liberty and Western consumerism. The two seemed to go together. So when the Soviet Empire collapsed after 1989, media moguls were quick to claim the credit. Looking back from 1997, Ted Turner, then still in charge of CNN, boasted: 'We have played a positive role. Since the creation of CNN, the Cold War has ended, the conflicts in Central America have come to a halt, and peace has come to South Africa.'[22]

But, like other revolutions in communications, television proved to

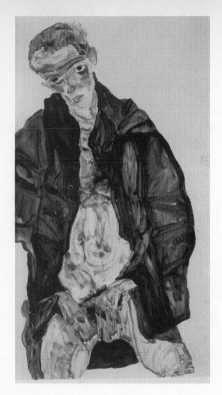

Egon Schiele, 'Self-portrait in Black Cloak, Masturbating', 1911 (*Albertina, Vienna*)

Tracey Emin, 'Everyone I Have Ever Slept With, 1963–1995', 1995
(*photograph by Stephen White; reproduced by permission of Jay Jopling/ White Cube, London*)

be a double-edged sword. It exposed the inability of the Soviets to control Afghanistan, but it also exposed the inability of the Americans to control Vietnam. It advertised the attractions of consumerism, but also laid bare its excesses. If it inspired the serfs of socialist command-economies to rattle their chains, it also inspired the children of its beneficiaries to bite the hands that fed them. For the post-1945 generation which grew to maturity in the 1960s, modernism had become complacent, middle-aged and – fatal adjective – boring. The eruption of youth culture thrust reason to one side. If it acquired a brief political tinge in 1968 and if its exponents have always been prone to striking moralizing postures of a vaguely leftist kind, at the heart of youth culture is anarchic hedonism. Significantly, its preferred medium has been music. Also revealing is the strong emphasis on narcotics, to facilitate escape from mundane reality and its illusory values to the 'wonder world of the night'. So massive is the purchasing power of young people (those aged 14 to 25 account for over 70 per cent of record sales, for example),[23] that what was still a marginal group as recently as the 1950s is now the driving force in consumerist culture.

There has also been a corresponding reaction to the culture of reason at a more intellectual level, in the shape of the strands known collectively as 'postmodernism'. Thankfully, there is no space to investigate this richly various – and contradictory – phenomenon. It must suffice to assert that all postmodernists have in common a rejection of grand narrative, teleology and rationalism. They squarely belong with the passionate paradigm, in a line which has stretched in this lecture back to *fin de siècle*, romanticism and the baroque. But, as before, this was not just another spin of the cycle's wheel, but a dialectical progression. It may be assumed that Nietzsche, even in his more nihilist moods, would not have accepted Jacques Derrida's radical assault on the possibility of knowledge and 'logocentrism' (although he would certainly have expressed himself with greater cogency and clarity than his postmodern successors). The trend towards extremes, however, has continued. Instead of Aubrey Beardsley's decadent *fin de siècle* homoeroticism, we have Gilbert and George's *New Horny Pictures*, consisting of representations of the artists framed by enlarged telephone-kiosk-advertisements for male prostitutes, or their 'fundamental pictures':

SPUNK BLOOD PISS SHIT SPIT	BLOOD	LAVATORY
BLOOD TEARS SPUNK PISS	PISS ON BLOOD	BLOOD ON BLOOD
PISSED	BLOOD ON PISS	SPIT ON SHIT
BLOODY MOONING	FRONT AND BACK PISS	BLOODY FAITH
IN THE SPIT	SPUNK MOONING	SPIT BLIND
PISS ON US	BLOODY NAKED	BLOOD AND PISS
PISS FAITH	BLOODY CARRIERS	SPUNK AND TEARS
PISS GUNS	OUR PISS	SPAT ON
BLOOD ON SHIT	PISS PISTOLS	PISS PLANTS
PISS ON PISS	SHIT AND PISS	BLOOD AND PISS HEADS
HOLY PISS	BLOODY WORLD	SPUNK ON BLOOD
SPUNK	BLOODY SHIT HOUSE	SPIT ON PISS
PISS PISS PISS	PISS MOONING	SPUNK ON US

Instead of Egon Schiele's *Self-portrait in Black Cloak, Masturbating* (1911), we have Tracey Emin's tent, whose walls are emblazoned with the names of 'All the people I have ever slept with' (the title of the work). This kind of contrast could be repeated at will. Perhaps every age gets the culture of passion it deserves. As postmodernism denies the possibility of objective standards, it must be left to the individual to determine whether these most recent works of art represent aesthetic advance.

Notes and References

1 Quoted in Naomi Klein, *No Logo* (London, 2000), p. 116.

2 Quoted in Rolf Toman (ed.), *Die Kunst des Barock: Architektur, Skulptur, Malerei* (Cologne, 1997), p. 286.

3 Quoted in Denis Hollier (ed.), *A New History of French Literature* (Cambridge, Mass., 1989), p. 383.

4 Quoted in Glyndon G. Van Deusen, *Sieyès: His Life and His Nationalism* (New York, 1932), p. 75, n. 3.

5 Quoted in Mona Ozouf, 'Revolutionary Religion', in François Furet and Mona Ozouf (eds), *A Critical Dictionary of the French Revolution* (Cambridge, Mass., 1989), p. 564.

6 Quoted in Robert Brécy, *The Revolution in Song* (Paris, 1988), p. 151.

7 Quoted in Isaiah Berlin, 'The Counter-Enlightenment', in idem, *Against the Current: Essays in the History of Ideas* (London, 1979), p. 8.

8 Johann Wolfgang von Goethe, 'Von deutscher Baukunst', reprinted in Johann Gottfried Herder (ed.), *Von deutscher Art und Kunst* (1773), ed. Edna Purdie (Oxford, 1924), p. 129.

9 *Ibid.*, p. 123.
10 Jean Jacques Rousseau, *The Confessions*, ed. J.M. Cohen (London, 1953), p. 190.
11 Quoted in Helmut Börsch-Supan, *Caspar David Friedrich* (Munich, 1980), p. 8.
12 Quoted in Hans-Ulrich Wehler, *Deutsche Gesellschaftsgeschichte*, vol. II: *Von der Reformära bis zur industriellen und politischen 'Deutschen Doppelrevolution' 1815–1848/49* (Munich, 1987), p. 207.
13 Quoted in Linda Nochlin, *Realism* (London, 1971), p. 23.
14 *Ibid.*, p. 41.
15 Stewart Spencer and Barry Millington (eds), *Selected Letters of Richard Wagner* (London, 1987), p. 243.
16 Martin Gregor-Dellin and Dietrich Mack (eds), *Cosima Wagner's Diaries*, 2 vols (London, 1978), p. 623.
17 Quoted in Ronald Hayman, *Nietzsche: A Critical Life* (London, 1995), p. 163.
18 Quoted in Martin Jay, 'From Modernism to Post-modernism', in T.C.W. Blanning (ed.), *The Oxford Illustrated History of Modern Europe* (Oxford, 1996), p. 262.
19 *Ibid.*, p. 267.
20 David Watkin and Tilman Mellinghoff, *German Architecture and the Classical Ideal 1740–1840* (London, 1987), p. 178.
21 Nikolaus Pevsner, *An Outline of European Architecture*, 5th edn (Harmondsworth, 1957), p. 285. The first edition was published in 1943.
22 Quoted in Armand Mattelart, *Networking the World: The World 1794–2000* (Minneapolis and London, 2000), p. 95.
23 Axel Körner, 'Culture', in Mary Fulbrook (ed.), *Europe since 1945* (Oxford, 2001), p. 159.

Notes on Contributors

Christopher Andrew is Professor of Contemporary History and President and Fellow of Corpus Christi College. He teaches twentieth-century political history and international relations with particular reference to the role and influence of intelligence agencies. His publications include *Secret Service: The Making of the British Intelligence Community, Codebreaking and Signals Intelligence*; *KGB: The Inside Story* (with Oleg Gordievsky); *Instructions from the Centre: Top Secret Files on KGB Foreign Operations 1975–1985*; *More Instructions from the Centre: Top Secret Files on KGB Global Operations 1975–1985*; *For the President's Eyes Only: Secret Intelligence and the American Presidency from Washington to Bush*; *Eternal Vigilance? Fifty Years of the CIA* (with Rhodri Jeffreys-Jones); and *The Mitrokhin Archive. Vol I: The KGB in Europe and the West*.

Tim Blanning is Professor of Modern European History in the Faculty of History at Cambridge University and a Fellow of Sidney Sussex College. He teaches European history in the eighteenth and nineteenth centuries and specialises in political and cultural history of Britain, France and Germany and the Habsburg monarchy. His publications include *The French Revolution in Germany, The Origins of the French Revolutionary Wars, Joseph II, The French Revolutionary Wars 1787–1802, The French Revolution: Class War or Culture Clash?*, and *The Culture of Power and the Power of Culture: Old Regime Europe 1660–1789*.

Peter Clarke is Professor of Modern History in the Faculty of

History at Cambridge University and Master of Trinity Hall. He teaches modern British political history and his publications include *Lancashire and the New Liberalism, Labour and Social Democrats, The Keynesian Revolution in the Making, The Keynesian Revolution and its Economic Consequences, Hope and Glory* and *The Cripps Version: The Life of Sir Stafford Cripps.*

Rosamond McKitterick is Professor of Early European History in the Faculty of History in Cambridge University and a Fellow of Newnham College. She is a historian of continental Europe from the fifth to the tenth centuries, teaching political, religious, cultural, social, intellectual and economic themes. She specialises in the Carolingian period, the Vikings in Europe and British history from the fifth to the tenth centuries. Her publications include *The Frankish Kingdoms under the Carolingians, The Carolingians and the Written Word, Books, Scribes and Learning in the Frankish Kingdoms, Sixth to Ninth Centuries, The Frankish Kings and Culture in the Early Middle Ages,* and, with Roland Quinault, *Edward Gibbon and Empire.*

Quentin Skinner is Regius Professor of History at Cambridge University and a Fellow of Christ's College. He is a historian of intellectual history and teaches philosophy of history, modern political philosophy, history of political philosophy and early-modern intellectual history. His publications include *The Foundations of Modern Political Thought* (two volumes), *Liberty before Liberalism, Reason and Rhetoric in the Philosophy of Hobbes* and *Visions of Politics* (three volumes).

Jonathan Steinberg was formerly Reader in Modern European History at the Faculty of History at Cambridge University and is now the Walter H. Annenberg Professor of Modern European History at the University of Pennsylvania and Chair of the Department of History. He was the principal author of the report, 'The Deutsche Bank and its Gold Transactions during the Second World War' (1999). He is the author of *Yesterday's Deterrent: Tirpitz and the Birth of the German Battle Fleet* (1965), *Why Switzerland?* (1976; 2nd ed. 1996) and *All or Nothing: The Axis and the Holocaust, 1941–1943* (1990).

John A. Thompson is Senior Lecturer in American History in the Faculty of History at Cambridge University and a Fellow of St Catharine's College, Cambridge. His chief interest is in twentieth-century American history, and his publications include *Reformers and War: American Progressive Publicists and the First World War* (1987) and *Woodrow Wilson* (2002).

Clive Trebilcock is Reader in Modern Economic and Social History in the Faculty of History at Cambridge University. He is also a Fellow and Director of Studies in History at Pembroke College. He is a business historian, but also teaches nineteenth and twentieth-century European and Japanese economic and social history. His publications include *The Vickers Brothers: Armament and Enterprise*, *The Industrialisation of the Continental Powers*, *Phoenix Assurance and the Development of British Insurance* (two volumes) and, with Peter Clarke, *Understanding Decline*.

Sir Tony Wrigley is Emeritus Professor in Economic and Social History in the Faculty of History at Cambridge University and a Fellow and former Master of Corpus Christi College, Cambridge. A demographic historian, his publications include *The Population History of England 1541–1871* (with R.S. Schofield), *People, Cities and Wealth* and *Continuity, Chance and Change*. He was appointed President of the British Academy in 1997 and retired in 2001.

Index